The Next Generation
of Pastoral Leaders

OTHER BOOKS IN THE
EMERGING MODELS OF PASTORAL
LEADERSHIP SERIES

The Changing Face of Church:
Emerging Models of Parish Leadership
by Marti R. Jewell and David A. Ramey

Parish Life Coordinators:
Profile of an Emerging Ministry
by Kathy Hendricks

Pastoring Multiple Parishes:
An Emerging Model of Pastoral Leadership
by Mark Mogilka and Kate Wiskus

Shaping Catholic Parishes:
Pastoral Leaders in the 21st Century
edited by Carole Ganim

The Next Generation of Pastoral Leaders

WHAT THE CHURCH NEEDS TO KNOW

Dean R. Hoge and Marti R. Jewell

◇◇◇

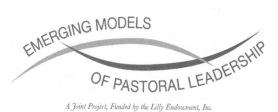

A Joint Project, Funded by the Lilly Endowment, Inc.

LOYOLAPRESS.
A JESUIT MINISTRY
Chicago

Partnering for Pastoral Excellence

    National Catholic Young Adult Ministry Association

LOYOLA PRESS.
A JESUIT MINISTRY

3441 N. Ashland Avenue
Chicago, Illinois 60657
(800) 621-1008
www.loyolapress.com

Cover silhouette: iStock/Kirsty Pargeter
Cover design by Kathryn Seckman Kirsch and Mia McGloin
Interior design by Maggie Hong

Library of Congress Cataloging-in-Publication Data
Hoge, Dean R., 1937-2008.
  The next generation of pastoral leaders : what the church needs to know / by Dean R. Hoge and Marti R. Jewell.
     p. cm.
  Includes bibliographical references.
  ISBN-13: 978-0-8294-2650-2
  ISBN-10: 0-8294-2650-7
  1. Catholic Church—United States—Clergy—Appointment, call, and election—Public opinion. 2. Lay ministry—Catholic Church—Public opinion. 3. Christian leadership—Catholic Church—Public opinion. 4. Catholic Church--United States—Public opinion. 5. Public opinion—United States. 6. Catholics—United States—Attitudes. 7. Young adults—United States—Attitudes. I. Jewell, Marti R. II. Title.
  BX1912.H593 2010
  262'.02—dc22
                                                    2009043612

Printed in the United States of America
10 11 12 13 14 15 Versa 10 9 8 7 6 5 4 3 2 1

Dedication

To a man who was truly a gentleman and a scholar.
Many of us called him friend.

Dean R. Hoge
1937–2008

Contents

Preface

Most Reverend Joseph W. Estabrook
Auxiliary Bishop
Archdiocese for the Military Services, USA

John Westerhoff authored a book entitled *Will Our Children Have Faith?* This present volume, *The Next Generation of Pastoral Leaders: What the Church Needs to Know* by Dean Hoge and Marti Jewell, presents material that might turn that question around: "Will our faith have children?" The hard realities presented in this book are challenging and compelling. It's imperative that the current church leadership listen and respond to its young people for the sake of the Church and the future of its mission.

The authors provide hope and a viable way to evangelize our young adults, whom their study reveals to be searching for what the Gospel of Jesus and his Catholic Church in particular have to offer. But the leaders of the Church today must capture their imaginations early with the challenge of what it means to live as true disciples in our secular world.

Very often our impression of young adults is that they spend a majority of their time connected to mobile devices. Hoge and Jewell present findings that indicate there is more to the life of a young adult than texting and online social networking. The findings indicate that young adults today do indeed value human relationships, seek ways to serve others, and give serious thought toward discerning how

God might be calling them to a more generous living out of their faith.

Young adults today have grown up in a more global world. They tend to think beyond borders and assess how their daily living impacts the lives of others. All of this is a result of education, travel, and participation in service projects combined with prayerful reflection. These lived experiences along with the present uncertain economic realities predispose Catholic young adults to look beyond themselves in order to build up the Body of Christ.

Young adults are looking for their place in the Church. They desire to know more about Catholicism. They have a respect for the sacred. They have many gifts to offer the Church, and they possess a sense of enthusiasm along with the ability to reach others through technology and personal invitation. They care about the future of the Church.

The Catholic Church in the United States must reflect on these findings and examine, along with Catholic young adults, what it means to truly engage them. Currently, young adults find it difficult to find pathways to full-time ministry. They are seeking mentors and having trouble finding them. They possess gifts that will serve the needs of others, but the community of faith is doing little to help them recognize, explore, and foster those gifts. The church must reflect on and move toward reaching out to Catholic young adults. We cannot sit in our offices waiting for them to come to us. We need to be present in their online world as well as in their lived experiences.

The Church must not only present authentic models of discipleship; we must also help Catholic young adults actually practice discipleship. In doing so we encourage them to find their place. Catholic young adults are graced with gifts that point to the presence of Christ here on earth and in the Kingdom of God. This book calls us to be in relationship with Catholic young adults so that together all of us may vibrantly pass on the faith, which ultimately is a gift to be shared.

Introduction

The American Catholic Church is re-evaluating some institutional practices. This is necessary because of recent social changes and trends. Above all, Catholics in America are more educated and affluent than ever in history, and they are now fully integrated into American society. They are growing in numbers at the same time that the priesthood is declining. Under these circumstances, automatic continuation of all past institutional practices is not the most hopeful plan for the future. Rather, we need to reflect on the mission of the Church, how we can serve that mission, and what innovations in policies would serve that mission.

In a 2003 survey of American Catholics, they were asked what are the most important problems now facing the Catholic Church. From a list of twelve problems drawn from Catholic media, the respondents picked their priorities. The top three were the crisis of sexual abuse by priests, the shortage of priests and sisters, and the absence of young adults in parish life. This book sheds light on the second and third—the shortage of pastoral leaders and the attitudes of young adults.

In 2005, a coalition of six Catholic organizations asked the Lilly Endowment for a grant to plan for the future of parish life. The six were the National Association for Lay Ministry, the Conference for Pastoral Planning and Council Development, the National Association of Church Personnel Administrators, the National Association of Diaconate Directors, the National Catholic Young Adult Ministry Association, and the National

Federation of Priests Councils. The Lilly Endowment made a significant grant to support research, consultations, and meetings in a program called Emerging Models of Pastoral Leadership. Marti Jewell was named project director.

The collaborating organizations of the project felt a need for new surveys of young adults to assess their attitudes about serving the Church in ministry positions in the future. In particular they wanted to hear young adults tell what encouraged them or discouraged them when they thought about becoming lay ministers, priests, sisters, or deacons. The Emerging Models Project asked Dean Hoge if he would help carry out new research, and he suggested a Hoge-Jewell collaboration. Work began in summer 2006. We recruited an advisory committee to make initial decisions about the most useful research. The committee met in September and recommended two surveys, one of Catholic college students and one of young adults not currently college students. The surveys were to be supplemented by numerous personal interviews and focus groups, all of which were about the opinions of young adults about future ministry and the Church.

In spring 2007 we carried out an online survey of Catholic college students and of young adults known to diocesan offices. By design, this survey was not a random sample of all Catholic college students, but only those students known to Catholic campus ministries and Newman Centers in a random sample of colleges—including Catholic, public, and private non-Catholic colleges and universities. The result was a survey of Catholic college students who were at least minimally involved in Church life or in campus ministry in some way.

The survey of nonstudents was sent to young adults twenty to thirty-nine years old known to diocesan offices, usually offices of young adult ministry or parish life. We wanted to survey persons not attending college, either those who never attended or who were now alumni. To do the survey, we phoned a random sample of American dioceses, one in each episcopal region, and inquired about what kind of e-mail lists they had available or could compile. The resulting survey was mainly of persons in their late twenties or thirties, most of whom were college alumni. While it had been hoped that there would be data from young adults who had not attended college, this did not prove to be the case; these young adults were not reached by or did not respond to the surveys. Information needed about their interest is left to further study.

Ninety-three percent of the respondents in the diocesan sample and 96 percent of the college sample were raised as Catholics. The college students (98 percent) were not married, while one-third of the diocesan sample were married. Twelve percent of the college sample and 6 percent of the diocesan sample described themselves as Latino/a. Where responses differed significantly, based on any of these factors, it is noted in the text.

We also interviewed 55 in person or by phone, asking them about their views about possible future ministry and more broadly about their attitudes about Church life and the future of American Catholicism. In this group were thirteen people already working in lay ministry. All the interviews were taped and transcribed. We also carried out four focus groups. Details of the research method are given in the appendix.

This book summarizes our findings. We have tried to be as exact and reliable as possible, preferring not to voice our own viewpoints on the many findings and the issues they raised. Our purpose was to describe the situation in the year 2007 as reliably and as free of bias as possible. Whether the news is good or bad in each instance is for others to decide. We asked three people to read our report and write their own commentaries about our findings and implications for the future. Their reflections are included here at the end of the book. What has caused young adults to answer the way they do or what the Church will do because of their viewpoints is left to the reader to decide.

Acknowledgments

We benefited from good help from many people. Our advisory committee was composed of Kate DeVries, Erin Duffy, Kimberly Greenburg, Ken Johnson-Mondragon, Lucien Roy, Kathy Schmitt, Jared Suire, and Sr. Eileen McCann. Kate, Erin, Kimberly, and Sr. Eileen carried out interviews and focus groups. Our online surveys were set up by Community IT Innovators. Claudia Penn and Janel Bakker transcribed interviews.

We thank the commentators who reflected on our findings and thought through their implications: Edward Hahnenberg, Paul Jarzembowski, and Rachel Hart Winter.

An invitation to young adults to participate in the survey was provided by the Most Reverend Blase Cupich, bishop of the Diocese of Rapid City.

Finally, we thank the nineteen campus ministers and twelve diocesan offices who helped us with the online survey samples. Their names are listed in the appendix.

We hope that this book is of genuine service to the American Catholic community in planning for its future.

Dean Hoge
Marti Jewell

State of the Church in the Twenty-first Century

Here's the scene. It is 1965, and the American bishops have just returned from the closing session of the Second Vatican Council. They are looking into the future using the eyes of the 1950s, expecting growth and vitality. What they could not know was that the coming decade would change their plans.

The bishops had no way to know that the years of the 1960s, with their civil rights advances, cultural revolution, and feminist revolution would be a turning point not only for American Catholicism but for all religious groups in America. The 1960s ushered in many changes, some of which have become permanent.

Today, more than forty years later, we can look back at those changes. Nobody foresaw them. Everyone was taken by surprise. The trends since then strongly influence what the American Catholic Church can and cannot do in the future. What trends are we talking about? We look first at trends in the American Catholic community, then at trends in the institutional Church.

Trends in the Catholic Community

Catholicism in America is growing steadily. At present the rate of growth is about 8 percent to 12 percent per decade (Hoge and Wenger, 15). This is mainly due to immigration, since the rate of immigration to the United States is now at an all-time high. The importance of immigration is both in the number of people coming in and in the larger families of immigrants. The major growth is in Hispanics. The percentage of American Catholics who are Hispanic is growing. The exact figure is difficult to know, but it lies somewhere between 25 and 35 percent today, and it is rising.

For all Catholics, the levels of education and affluence have risen, and they will continue to rise in the future. In the 1960s, less than 10 percent of all Catholics had achieved college degrees; in contrast, it is about 30 percent today (Davidson 2005, 12). The biggest gains in educational level have been among women.

The level of disposable wealth since the 1960s has doubled for Catholics, just as it has for other Americans. Along with increased wealth have come new attitudes about expected standards of living. Owning a house complete with appliances, air conditioning, and a two-car garage used to be seen as a hoped-for achievement of the middle adult years, but now it has come to be seen as normal for people in their thirties, even if two paychecks in the family are needed to maintain this level. The sense of entitlement among young adults is also higher than ever before in American history. What used to be good enough is no longer felt to be good enough (Wuthnow, 34).

Catholic young adults are more integrated into all of American society than ever in history. They go to college side-by-side with non-Catholics, they work side-by-side with non-Catholics, and they choose about half of their marriage partners from non-Catholics. The barriers that Catholics felt a half century ago between themselves and other Americans have fallen away. Today Catholic politicians run for office in America alongside Protestant politicians, and what religion they belong to is uninteresting to most voters.

Polls measuring anti-Catholic feelings in the 1950s found fairly high levels among American Protestants, but the feelings began fading away after the presidency of John F. Kennedy, and by the 1970s they were so low that pollsters no longer measured them. Today anti-Catholic feelings in the American population are very weak. A majority of justices in the Supreme Court are Catholics, and the chaplain to the U.S. House of Representatives is Catholic. To most Americans, it doesn't matter.

Young adult Catholics are the most educated, affluent, cultural-conscious, well-traveled, and confident of any in American history. Today a few more Catholics of college age, percentage-wise, are attending college than is true for Protestants, according to annual nationwide freshman surveys. Especially among the college-educated, they have very few feelings of defensiveness or self-consciousness about their Catholicism. Overall income levels of Protestants and Catholics in America are similar.

A final trend is worth noting. It occurs among both Catholics and non-Catholics. Americans are slowly losing trust in their large institutions. Levels of trust today are lower than several decades ago, as polls show (D'Antonio et al, 29; Hoge and Wenger, 8). This includes the levels of faith in Congress, the executive branch, large corporations, the media, public schools, and organized religion. Young adults feel less trust in these basic institutions than older adults, and the overall shift affects how young persons look at churches and Church teachings.

Trends in the Institutional Church

While the number of Catholics is rising, the number of priests in the United States is falling. The priesthood has been declining for three decades. The current rate of decline is 12 percent to 14 percent per decade. The ranks of the religious priests are thinning more rapidly than the ranks of the diocesan; religious priests are declining at about 20 percent per decade, while the diocesan are declining at about 9 percent (CARA, 2). The main cause of decline is not that a large number of priests are resigning; the resignation rate is low. Rather, the decline occurs because too few men are being ordained each year. At present, ordinations are between 35 percent and 45 percent of what are needed each year to keep the priesthood numbers constant. Stated plainly, we need at least a doubling of ordinations each year to maintain the Church as we have known it. But a doubling of ordinations seems impossible.

Efforts to encourage more men into the priesthood in recent years have had limited results. In spite of new programs and initiatives, the number of seminarians has not increased; on the contrary, the number has receded slowly at the rate of about 4 percent to 7 percent per decade. Yet in the past seven years there has been little or no decline—so perhaps the situation is stabilizing.

The question is often asked, can we increase the number of ordinations by working harder at encouraging young men to become priests? Recent experience is not encouraging, and the most realistic prospect is that ordinations will not increase in the next decade. Meanwhile the laity-to-priest ratio will increase. In 1965 it stood at 800 laity per priest, and in 2007 it was 1,550 per priest, a number that includes all priests, diocesan and religious, whether actively serving in parishes or not. The plentiful number of priests that American Catholics experienced in the 1960s and 1970s will not return, and the Church must develop new forms of leadership in its parishes. This, if our experience is any guide, is not good news for either the laity or the priests. Everyone wants more priests. The laity want more priestly services, the priests want more colleagues to share the ministerial load, and the bishops want more priests to staff their parishes.

How about the number of parishes? In the decades when the number of Catholics increased, did the number of parishes in the United States also increase? No. The number of parishes has remained constant since 1975 and is only now beginning to decline. As a result, the average size of a parish has risen. In 2007 the average parish size was 3,400 members, or about 1300 families (CARA, 2). Indications are this figure will continue to rise.

Inevitably, not every parish can have a resident priest pastor. Back in 1965 only 3 percent had no resident pastor, but then the number grew. In 1995 it was 11 percent, and in 2007 it was 17 percent. The number is greater in the Midwest and the West than in the Northeast and the South. It is certain to grow everywhere in the years ahead.

Today more and more priests are being asked to pastor more than one parish. In a 2005 survey of priests a few years out of seminary—an average of seven years out—54 percent of the diocesan priests and 18 percent of the religious priests were pastors. Of the priests who were now pastors, 36 percent of the diocesan and 20 percent of the religious were responsible for more than one parish (Hoge, 48).

Downward trends in the Catholic women's communities are more dramatic than in the priesthood. The number of sisters has declined about 15 percent to 18 percent per decade since the 1960s. This decline is continuing year by year. The values and viewpoints of young American women today are such that few of them are willing to make this lifetime commitment. The women's revolution since the 1960s has widened the occupational and leadership possibilities for American women, encouraging young Catholic women to enter other service professions besides the sisterhood. As a result the horizons of young American women are wider than ever. Therefore the most prudent assumption for Church leaders to make for planning for the future would be that the number of sisters will continue to decline.

Growth in Lay Ministry

Professional lay ministers, called lay ecclesial ministers, have increased dramatically since the 1990s. We need to be clear about the definition. A professional lay minister is a trained person working full-time or part-time in a formal, recognized position in a parish, not including Catholic school teachers, support staff, or business personnel. They include vowed religious persons, i.e., those who are not ordained.

We are fortunate to have a series of three nationwide surveys of professional lay ministers, done in 1990, 1997, and 2005. These surveys included only the lay ministers working twenty hours a week or more. Between 1990 and 2005, the number of such persons in the United States increased an estimated 42 percent, with most of the increase coming in the early 1990s (DeLambo 2005, 44). This is a major recent innovation in Catholic parish life. The latest studies indicate more than 31,000 lay ecclesial ministers are serving in parishes.

The percentage of these lay ministers who are women religious dropped from 41 percent to 16 percent, reflecting the dwindling number of women religious in service. Most of the other lay ministers were lay women. The percentage of men in the samples was only 15 percent in 1990 and 20 percent in 2005. Hispanics made up 8.1 percent of lay ecclesial ministers. The principal ministry categories were religious educators and general pastoral ministers, followed by youth ministers and music ministers. The median age of laypersons in lay ministry (not including religious) rose from forty-five to fifty-two in fifteen years. (DeLambo, 46). And the level of education of lay ministers is high. In 2005, 48 percent had a master's degree or more. The average salary for full-time lay ministers was $35,261.

The United States Council of Catholic Bishops issued a statement on lay ministries, *Co-Workers in the Vineyard of the Lord*, in 2005. It called laypersons into ecclesial ministry, saying that their role and ministry is complementary to that of the ordained ministry and that the two must work together in collaboration (*Co-Workers*, 15). The document describes contractual agreements that it recommends using when hiring lay ministers, and it suggests a public ceremony or liturgy to commission new lay ecclesial ministers when beginning work in a parish.

The growth in the number of lay ministers is happening at the same time that the number of priests is declining, but lay ecclesial ministry has a theological warrant apart from that.

The status of laypersons was set forth in the documents of Vatican II as being partners in ministry on the basis of their baptism (Lakeland, 42). That is, lay ministers are not just "substitutes for priests" when priests are not available, or "the apostolate of the second string." They are ministers in their own right, and the growth of lay ministries is a belated theological recognition of the proper role of the laity in parish life.

Emerging Adulthood

It is important to mention a basic change in how Americans view the human life cycle. Whereas before the 1960s, Americans saw adolescence feeding directly into adulthood when the young persons graduated, got married, and had children in their twenties, today it is understood that there is an additional chapter in human life. Researchers call it "emerging adulthood," and it extends from the teenage years into the twenties and early thirties. Young adults today are postponing marriage and childbirth; the average age of marriage today in America is twenty-seven, up from twenty-one in 1950 (Arnett 2004, 4). The average age of having a first child (for persons who marry) is about twenty-eight, up from twenty-two in 1950. They are also postponing long-term commitments to jobs and churches.

Young adults today feel entitled to make their own decisions about their lives. They are not motivated to do anything, including going to Mass, out of obligation. They ask, "What obligation?" "Who says?" A majority of Catholic young people believe that moral decisions are ultimately up to them, and that this is proper. They do not believe that the Church's magisterium knows the mind of God on all moral questions;

rather, moral questions are best approached through serious reflection by laity and clergy working together (D'Antonio, et al., ch. 6).

Young adult Catholics are quite ecumenical in their religious views. The vast majority believe that other religions besides Catholicism are valid. In a 2003 survey, 90 percent of Catholics up to the age of forty-two agreed that "If you believe in God, it doesn't really matter which religion you belong to" (D'Antonio, et al., 31). Put simply, the boundaries separating young adult Catholics from young adult Protestants in America are down, and people in both groups feel goodwill and openness toward the other.

In sum: the years of the twenties are commonly seen today as a privileged young adult time for training, wide experiences, and exploration of options. Not every young person has this luxury, since many of them need to earn money or care for children they already gave birth to. "Emerging adulthood" occurs mainly among the middle-class or upper-class young people.

Summary

This chapter has enumerated changes in the Catholic population and the Church since Vatican II. Mostly it is good news. Wealth is up, education is up, anti-Catholicism is down, feelings of well-being as Catholics are up, and feelings of defensiveness against other Americans are down. There is much to celebrate.

However, from another point of view, there is bad news. Not everything can continue as it was. Social change has put pressure on many of the policies and practices of the institutional Church, particularly in regard to the structure of parish life. Some of them, inevitably, will not continue strong. Previous forms of parish leadership are certainly on the list for re-evaluation, and any research clarifying the task will help.

In the chapters that follow, we will look at the 2007 research on young adults to see their visions of the future of the Church and their possible participation in the Church's ministry.

2

Interest in Lay Ecclesial Ministry

I am very interested in possible full-time work as a lay minister serving the Catholic Church so that I can make a difference in people's lives by being an instrument of Jesus. I would love to teach people about the Sacraments, about the Rosary, about St. Michael, in order for them to adore, worship, and know our Eucharistic Lord more fully.

A man in his 30s

It is my calling from the Lord to work with the youth in my community. In teaching CCD and youth ministry, I have become aware of my gifts of preaching and evangelization. If the opportunity to work full-time in a long-term capacity presented itself, I would seriously consider it.

A woman in her 30s

I am interested in full-time work as a lay minister serving the Catholic Church because I can think of no better way to use the gifts God has given me than to give them back to him in joyful service to His Church and people. I feel it is certainly where I am called. In all the experiences I've had with ministry, and especially music ministry within the Church, I have found a sense of peace

and joy that I can only explain as the feeling of knowing
I am exactly where God wants me to be, doing exactly
what he wants me to be doing.

A man in his 20s

How many young Catholics today are interested in seriously considering future work as lay ministers? Why or why not? Our surveys included a series of questions, beginning with this:

"The Catholic Church in America is hiring more and more
full-time lay church ministers. Have you ever seriously con-
sidered becoming a professional lay minister, such as
director of religious education, youth minister, campus
minister, music minister, or pastoral associate?"

Table 2.1 shows the results. About one-third of the college students said yes (35 percent of the men and 34 percent of the women), as did about one-half of the people in the diocesan sample (55 percent of the men and 50 percent of the women).

If people said no, would they be interested later but not now? For the majority, yes. As the second item in the table indicates, a majority are leaving the door open to lay ministry later. Only about one-fourth of the people uninterested now said that they will never be interested. In short, the prevailing option is to keep the future open.

We asked the third question in Table 2.1 because some Catholics see lay ministry as an occupation for only a short time, not as a lifelong profession. How many of our respondents have this view? As the table shows, the college students and the diocesan sample had different opinions. The

Table 2.1

Interest in Full-Time Lay Ministry (in percents)

Here are some questions about your future vocation or occupation. The Catholic Church in America is hiring more and more full-time lay church ministers. Have you ever seriously considered becoming a professional lay minister, such as director of religious education, youth minister, campus minister, or pastoral associate?

	Student Sample		Diocesan Sample	
	Males	Females	Males	Females
Yes	35	34	55	50
No	45	50	37	39
Don't know	20	16	8	11

(if "no" or "don't know":) Which of these is closest to your attitude?

I doubt if I will ever be interested	28	20	27	28
I may be interested later, but not now	51	54	49	53
Unsure	21	26	24	19

(if "yes" on the first question:) Which of these is closest to your attitude?

I am interested in a long-term occupation in ministry	28	24	66	53
I am interested now, but only temporarily, not for the long term	23	23	9	10
Unsure	49	54	25	37

(if "yes" on the first question:) Have you taken any of the following steps to explore this form of ministry? (check all that apply)

Spoke to friends about it	66	68	67	71
Spoke to parents or other relatives	49	46	51	52
Spoke to a priest, religious or lay minister	64	38	62	58
Spoke to a career counselor	8	5	14	10
Looked online for information	25	44	41	42
Asked for information from a vocation director	23	10	24	15

college students were uncertain what to say. Half of them said "unsure," and the others were split between having interest for the long term and having interest only for the short term. The diocesan-sample people were different; the majority were interested in a long-term occupation in ministry, and very few wanted to do it short-term only. The diocesan-sample respondents were more definite in their attitudes, with only about one-third saying "unsure." The diocesan sample had a higher level of interest in lay ministry over the long term, while the college students were fairly tentative.

If respondents said that they have seriously considered becoming a lay minister, they were asked if have they taken any steps to explore it. We asked about this to judge how serious their interest was. Most were quite serious. See the last item in Table 2.1. The majority were interested enough to speak to friends and to a priest, a religious, or a lay minister. In addition, half had spoken to a parent or other relative. Much less commonly they had looked online for information, asked for information from a vocation director, or spoken to a career counselor.

Comparing Students Active or Inactive in Campus Ministry

Our college sample is composed of students known to the campus ministry centers at their colleges. What if we had been able to survey a random sample of Catholics in these colleges, regardless of the students' involvement in any campus ministry? This sort of survey is difficult to do for a researcher, but we can see an approximation by looking at the Catholic students in our sample who do not participate in the campus ministry program. They are interesting to us, since the majority of Catholics at any college or university do not participate in Catholic campus ministries. Estimates of participation never go higher than 30 percent of all Catholic students, and usually they are much lower. If we look at the nonparticipants in our sample, we can get an approximate view of the attitudes of the other Catholics. Table 2.2 breaks down the student survey into three levels of participation in campus ministry—leaders, frequent participants, and non-participants.

The three columns in the table are clearly different. The student's level of involvement in the campus ministry is a strong predictor of interest in future lay ministry. Of the most active students, 52 percent have seriously considered lay ministry, while of the noninvolved, only 16 percent. The students less involved in campus ministry, even though they are interested in lay ministry, have taken fewer steps to explore this form of ministry.

Interested in What Type of Ministry?

Which specific types of lay ministry are most interesting to the respondents? Look at Table 2.3. It shows that three occupations are ahead of all the others: (1) youth minister or young adult minister, (2) religious educator, and (3) teacher or administrator in a Catholic school. All are forms of ministry to children or youth. This is an important finding: *these people want most of all to minister to children and youth.* They are also interested in teaching in Catholic schools. Many of them see teaching in Catholic schools as similar to youth ministry or young adult ministry (as shown by their comments).

The other ministry options are a bit less attractive—pastoral associate; campus, hospital, or prison minister; social action

Table 2.2

Interest in Lay Ministry, in Three Levels of Campus Ministry Involvement (in percents)

Here are some questions about your future vocation or occupation. The Catholic Church in America is hiring more and more full-time lay church ministers. Have you ever seriously considered becoming a professional lay minister, such as director of religious education, youth minister, campus minister, or pastoral associate?

	College Student Sample		
	Officer or leader	Participant	Not involved
Number of cases:	**(106)**	**(260)**	**(55)**
Yes	52	32	16
(if "no" or "don't know":) Which of these is closest to your attitude?			
I doubt if I will ever be interested	14	25	26
I may be interested later, but not now	67	52	41
Unsure	20	23	33
(if "yes" on the first question:) Which of these is closest to your attitude?			
I am interested in a long-term occupation in ministry	29	23	a
I am interested now, but only temporarily, not for the long term	24	23	a
Unsure	47	54	a
(if "yes" on the first question:) Have you taken any of the following steps to explore this form of ministry? (check all that apply)			
Spoke to friends about it	78	61	a
Spoke to parents or other relatives	55	45	a
Spoke to a priest, religious or lay minister	62	41	a
Spoke to a career counselor	4	7	a
Looked online for information	33	38	a
Asked for information from a vocation director	18	12	a

a = Not enough cases.

Table 2.3

Interest in Specific Types of Ministry (in percents)

Would you be seriously interested in full-time employment in these occupations? (check all that apply)

	Student Sample		Diocesan Sample	
	Males	Females	Males	Females
As a youth minister or young adult minister	61	77	83	69
As a religious educator	49	63	70	69
As a teacher or administrator in a Catholic school	57	73	58	58
As a pastoral counselor or spiritual director	41	35	52	35
As a pastoral minister or pastoral associate	25	17	47	32
As a campus, hospital, or prison minister	34	43	45	34
As a parish business administrator	16	20	35	20
As a social action minister	34	46	33	30
As a music minister or liturgist	31	49	30	25
As a hospital chaplain	21	10	15	11
As a parish nurse	2	7	1	6

minister; music minister; and so on. Among the respondents in the diocesan survey, men showed greater interest in these options than women, while among the college students, men and women were not much different.

We checked to see if the responses in Table 2.3 would vary according to college students' level of campus ministry involvement. There was little variation.

Table 2.4 summarizes why the respondents are interested or uninterested in becoming lay ministers. The top part of the table is reasons for being interested. The online survey listed eight possibilities, as shown in the table, and asked respondent

Table 2.4

Reasons For and Against Interest in Lay Ministry
(in percents)

We are interested in attitudes toward full-time lay ministry in the Catholic Church. Here are reasons people sometimes give for being interested. Whether or not you are personally interested, how important would each be to you? (check all that apply)

	Student Sample		Diocesan Sample	
	Males	Females	Males	Females
It is a response to God's call	81	79	76	82
It is an opportunity to help other people	69	85	70	82
It is an opportunity to teach and pass on the faith	63	64	68	72
It is an opportunity to live out my faith	63	75	66	75
It utilizes my gifts and talents	44	59	63	71
It is very meaningful	54	65	58	67
It helps me grow in holiness	49	49	47	57
It provides prestige	6	10	3	6

Here are reasons people sometimes give for not being interested in serving the Catholic Church as a lay minister. Whether or not you are personally interested, how influential would each of these factors be in discouraging you? (check all that apply)

	Student Sample		Diocesan Sample	
	Males	Females	Males	Females
The wages are too low	19	16	40	33
I have a different occupation in mind	65	57	36	40
It does not utilize my gifts and talents	20	24	30	34
It is only short-term, with no long-term future	14	15	23	24
It has too little job security	9	14	21	24
It is given too little respect	4	4	9	9
Too much education is required	4	5	8	7
I know too little about it to be interested	13	12	8	9

to check the ones that apply; they are listed in descending order of frequency.

The main motivations are from religious commitment—feeling a calling from God, desiring to help other people, desiring to teach and pass on the faith, and wanting to live out one's faith. These are religious, not secular or extrinsic, goals. The one nonreligious option that we offered in the survey, "it provides prestige," was almost never chosen. The respondents who are interested in lay ministry have devout, spiritual motivations.

The bottom part of Table 2.4 assesses the reasons for having no interest in lay ministry. What are the factors that block these people's interest? Here we see a difference between what the college students and the people in the diocesan sample said. The main discouraging factor for the college students was "I have a different occupation in mind," far ahead of any other consideration. It appears that we have surveyed these students at a time when the majority had already made occupational choices. The second most chosen factor for the college students was similar: "it does not utilize my gifts and talents." Did the responses in Table 2.4 vary according to the students' level of involvement in campus ministry? Not much.

The respondents in the diocesan sample saw things a bit differently. For them, three discouraging factors were the most important—and roughly equal: "the wages are too low," "I have a different occupation in mind," and "it does not utilize my gifts and talents." Unlike the students, these people were discouraged by the low wages. In addition, the diocesan respondents gave a bit more importance to "it does not utilize my gifts and talents," "it is only short-term, with no long-term future" and "it has too little job security."

We were surprised that the college student respondents were more committed to other occupations than the respondents in the diocesan sample, who average six years older. We expected that the older young adults would be more committed to their occupations. But they were not. Maybe some of them were finding their occupations to be meaningless. Maybe they were frustrated. Whatever the explanation, we see that many people out of college and in their twenties and thirties are open to making occupational changes.

Differences by Age and Ethnicity

We looked for age differences in both samples. Were younger respondents different from older ones? In the college-student sample, age differences were small, largely because the age range was small. The only difference in the student sample was that older students potentially interested in lay ministry had taken a few more steps of exploration; this is probably explainable by being a few years older. In the diocesan sample there were no important differences by age.

Were Latinos different from others? (See Table A.2 in the appendix.) Latinos were less likely to have attended college, and they were more interested in future lay ministry than other Catholics. Our survey does not explain why. Otherwise Latino versus non-Latino differences were small.

Part-Time Ministry

We need to add a note about part-time lay ministry. In the 2007 surveys, we chose not to ask about part-time jobs, since our main interest was in full-time ministry and we were limited in the number of questions we could ask. But from other research we know that interest in part-time jobs is higher than interest in full-time jobs. In a 1985 survey of college students, interest in part-time jobs was about 20 percent or 30 percent higher than in full-time lay ministry (Hoge, 190). Based on our interviews in 2007, the 20 percent to 30 percent figure seems about right again, and possibly even too low. We heard repeated mention of interest in part-time ministry. The pool of college students potentially interested in lay ministry, if we include part-time jobs, is somewhat larger than we found in our survey.

Reasons Given by Respondents for Their Interest or Lack of Interest

We asked all the respondents to tell us in their own words why they are interested or uninterested in lay ministry. Almost all the respondents wrote in opinions. We divided the samples according to whether the respondent had ever seriously considered lay ministry or not (as shown in Table 2.1, with *don't* included with *no*).

Let us consider the college students first. Their comments indicated that not all of them are still seriously interested today. Judging from the open-ended responses, about 135 are interested at the present time—whereas 146 said yes in the initial question. We categorized the opinions of the 135 in nine categories. See Table 2.5, first column.

How about persons in the diocesan sample? How many are interested today? Initially 230 persons said that they were once seriously interested in lay ministry, but we discovered from

Table 2.5

Written-in Reasons for Interest in Lay Ministry

(in percents; up to two codes in any response)

	College Sample	Diocesan Sample
Number of responses:	(135)	(172)
To share the faith, to spread the faith; to help others grow in the faith	38	28
To use my gifts (music, speech, teaching, working with children, etc.); I enjoy this kind of work	16	16
To serve the Church; to serve the Catholic community	15	13
To help me develop my faith; to live out my faith; to express my love of Christ	13	12
I have been inspired by other teachers; want to give back something to God	8	2
To serve God	7	15
To integrate my faith with the rest of my daily life	7	2
To help people	5	12
To follow God's call; I have been called	4	15

their written-in information that twenty-five of them were already working full-time as lay ministers. We removed them from the sample. We also removed thirty-four persons who said they were no longer interested, leaving 172 currently interested. Their responses are shown in Table 2.5, second column.

As the table depicts, the motivations are similar for the two samples. The most important motivation is the desire to share the faith and help others grow in the faith. Second most important is the desire to exercise one's gifts usefully, and third is the desire to serve the Church and the Catholic community. Persons in the diocesan sample made more mention of feeling a call from God, a desire to serve God, and a desire to help people. All of these motivations strike us as commendable.

Table 2.6

Written-in Reasons for No Interest in Lay Ministry
(in percents; up to two codes in any response)

	College Sample	Diocesan Sample
Number of responses:	(288)	(231)
I am committed to another career	42	29
I do not feel called	10	3
I don't have the gifts and talents; it doesn't use my gifts and talents	8	9
I am not strong enough in my faith	6	5
Pay is too low	5	29
It's not a fulfilling career to me; not interesting	4	3
I disagree with the Church on some issues	3	7
I am committed to my home and children	0	20
I don't know enough about it to be interested	7	5

These young people want to become lay ecclesial ministers for sound religious reasons.

How about persons not interested in lay ministry? Why not? In the college-student sample, an estimated 288 persons are not interested now. We coded their reasons in nine categories, shown in Table 2.6, first column. In the diocesan sample, about 198 are uninterested now, shown in the second column.

The comments the sample members wrote in match the responses on the online survey. For college students, the main disincentive was that they were already committed to another career. A second one—much smaller—was that they did not feel called. For the persons in the diocesan sample, there were three disincentives—low pay, being committed to another career, and being committed to home and children. In short, the diocesan-survey respondents were more concerned about income and family obligations.

In the written-in comments we encountered several cases of misinformation about lay ministry. A few respondents thought, for whatever reason, that lay ministry required celibacy or adherence to special rules about living arrangements. A different problem, much more widespread, was a lack of information about lay ecclesial ministry. Numerous respondents said they were unaware of these opportunities.

Written-in Expressions of Interest in Lay Ministry

Below we give some examples of the respondents' reasons for being interested in lay ministry, grouped according to the four most prevalent reasons: (1) to share the faith; (2) to use my gifts or because I enjoy this kind of work; (3) to serve the Church and the Catholic community; and (4) to help me develop my faith.

(1) To share the faith

College students' comments often tell of their interest in helping others—families, children, youth—about their faith:

> I am interested because it would bring me closer to my faith, and I would have the chance to spread the word of God to the future of the church—the young people in our world today.

> I am currently a Junior High Coordinator for Religious Education at my home parish, and I really enjoy sharing the balance, rationality, and spiritual and joyful aspects

of my faith with kids that would otherwise be moving on to tomorrow without knowing what exactly the Church teaches. I am interested in working as a lay minister, but before just jumping into it I would like to finish college and discern a vocation.

I want to be able to be part of building up God's kingdom. I believe that this means my life, either by profession or vocation (or both) needs to speak to that desire by my involvement in ministering to the needs of others.

Comments by persons in the diocesan sample:

I would be interested in possible full-time work as a lay minister because it provides me with an opportunity to pass on the importance of the Catholic faith, especially in today's "me" society. We live in a society where money comes before family, where the youth are uninterested in God. To be able to help place God first in people's lives would be fulfilling.

Jesus has called us to spread the gospel to all ends of the earth. We need strong marriages, families, and parishes in order to prepare people for the ministry of living the gospel. Lay ministers have an amazing calling and opportunity to share the gospel and preserve the faith of the Catholic Church.

My faith has given me lots of strength and I enjoy passing it on. Also, I have seen so many fruitless efforts to bring religion to youth by trying to make it hip and cool and "rock and rolly." I think this is effort misspent. While I think it is critical to demonstrate how our faith has real relevance, it is disconcerting to watch efforts to market it like they would a band or a candy bar. I also think that these efforts have led to what I call the panacea Jesus. I want to work in ministry to spread the word about our faith that is real and inspiring and based in everyday living.

(2) To use my gifts, or I enjoy this kind of work
College students:

My mom is a lay minister serving the Catholic Church, and she loves it! I have grown up in the Catholic Church, and my father is a deacon. I love working with little children and aiding in religious education. Doing things like this full-time would be a great joy to me. I love doing things that involve my faith and I would love to share that with others.

I am interested in eventually becoming a music minister or youth leader. I've always enjoyed working with high-school age students and help out at a conference similar to Steubenville every summer. I feel that music is my calling and would like to work with high school students with a worship band or choir for Masses.

I am currently a catechist and I love it. I feel that this occupation would be similar to that but only on a larger scale. I could seriously see myself working for the church in the future and utilizing my gifts to help others see and reach their faith and life potentials. I love helping people, and this would be a great way to put my faith and love into action.

Comments from the diocesan sample:

I am currently a substitute cantor and my wife is currently a substitute organist. We are most interested in music ministry and are hoping to find a permanent position playing at a Catholic church. I feel that a church's music ministry is important because it not only spreads support for music but also gives parishioners another form of prayer to utilize.

I feel I have a calling to work with youth or young adults. I have a passion for keeping our young people in the Catholic Church. I believe that I would be using my gifts if I worked in this ministry.

I have previous experience in campus and youth ministry. It is something that I have enjoyed thoroughly.

(3) To serve the Church and the Catholic community

Comments about serving the Church and the Catholic community are similar to comments about serving God. Here are some by college students:

I am interested because I feel it could be the best way I can serve the Lord and my community.

I'm interested because the Catholic Church has always been an important part of my life, and I feel called to give back and use my talents towards what I know to be one of the most worthy institutions I know.

I feel interested in possible work as a lay minister of some kind because my parish life is very important to me, and I also feel like I have a lot to offer.

From the diocesan sample:

Growing up in a parish community, I have seen many liturgical and social changes within the Church. Unfortunately with the shortage of priests I am realistic enough to see how things will eventually change within the faith community. More and more lay persons are called to become leaders within the community. I believe it is the responsibility of the lay community to give more than just alms and 20 hours of volunteer work a year. As a lay person I am investing my faith not only in the present relationship I have with my community, but also in the future.

My husband and I are currently looking at many different possibilities for our future. If God is calling one or both of us to work as a lay minister in the Church, we will. I feel called to help the Church in one way or another, whether it's a paid position or not, and whether it's casual or formal.

To serve the Church is to serve God, who should be number one in everything we do. This would be an opportunity to use the skills and talents that God gave me, to give back to him and others.

(4) To help me develop my faith

From college students:

I am searching for my vocation and plan to live a life in harmony with that call. I do not want to separate my faith life from my personal or professional life. I want to incorporate it all into myself so that I can live a life of commitment to God. Lay ministry is one way to integrate my faith life with the rest of my life.

I want to continue to live out my faith through my everyday work and to have a meaningful job.

Jobs in the Catholic Church would allow me to put my faith into active ministry. Thus my job would allow me to live out my faith through my daily work and would allow me the opportunity to share with others how I can easily live out my faith.

It is a wonderful environment to be in and it would help me to grow in my faith. And, eventually, it would be a great job to have with a family and to be an example to my children. It would be a good influence for them, especially in today's world where there are so many bad examples and things to influence children.

From the diocesan sample:

> I am serious about my vocation and see work within the Church as a place where I can grow as well as share with other people. I also see the Church as in desperate need of leadership, especially female, and see my gifts and talents being used well in this role.

> I have a strong desire to help others and to better live out my faith. The Catholic Church must reach out to her members and help those who are floundering. I want to help others see that there is a better way than the secular culture that prevails today.

> To grow closer to God via sharing my faith on a daily basis in a controlled setting. It is easier to be faithful and express religion in the religious setting, rather than being ridiculed out in the secular world.

Written-in Expressions of Barriers to Interest in Lay Ministry

The respondents described three main barriers to a future in lay ministry: (1) being committed to another career; (2) being committed to home and children; and (3) the pay is too low. Here are examples.

(1) Committed to another career

From college students:

> I am interested to a certain extent. I would love to work and serve the Catholic Church, but I have my heart set on becoming a nurse. I like fast-paced work.

My goal in life is to have a family. I think that by pursuing a career that utilizes my talents (engineering) I will be able to build a financial foundation to support a family. I don't want to delay my career by being a lay minister first, because I don't plan on working forever. I will probably leave my job when I have children.

I am not interested right now because I am pursuing a career in engineering, and I would not have time for such a position. Also, organization is not a strong skill of mine, and neither is dealing with large groups of people.

I do not feel called to this ministry at this time. I will be going on a medical mission as a nurse after I graduate, and I feel that my talents/skills can be used better in this way.

I have plans to work in the entertainment field, but I do hope I can use that at times as a way to spread God's word. Also, the amount of commitment to being a full-time lay minister would be too much to do. Part-time lay ministry, such as lector or server, would be much more desirable.

From the diocesan sample:

I am not interested because I just earned my graduate degree in school counseling and just began that career. Money is a factor as well as the hours. I think I would be required to work more evenings and weekends, which I am not willing to give up because I have a young family.

I am working in clinical research with cancer patients. I feel this is where I am currently called to be. I enjoy reaching out to others, but I am not very eloquent, so I prefer one-on-one ministry. My impression of lay ministry is that it reaches out to groups of people. That's not my calling at this time.

I am highly educated in teaching special needs children and want to continue my focus there. I prefer volunteering my time and talent to my church rather than being employed there.

I am already well-established (eight years as high school teacher) in a career that allows me to help others and work with youth. I feel that laity with solid Catholic values are desperately needed in our public schools to help guide our youth. I am currently very active and involved in youth retreat ministry and with middle school ministry at my parish, but I do this on a part-time, volunteer basis because of my work commitments.

(2) Committed to home and children

College students did not mention commitment to home and children as a barrier. Only the diocesan sample persons did. Here are examples:

At this time I am a stay-at-home mom and feel that I wouldn't be able to devote the time necessary to fulfill the requirements. I do strongly believe that in the future, with more time on my hands, I would consider lay ministry.

Currently I am uninterested. My primary focus is building a stable household for my family. I am considering a lay ministry position in the future, in approximately the same pattern as my father. He successfully raised three children and was able to retire early and move into a lay ministry position.

Not interested mainly because I am twenty-nine years old, content with my current job in an international non-profit organization, and about to start a family. However, I would also be hesitant in the future because my husband currently works for the Church and even he, as a man, is not respected as he should be. He works very long hours for very little recognition. As a lay woman in the Church, I feel that my contributions would be even less respected and valued.

Right now I have personally answered the call to the married life, and already have a child on the way. The possibility of ministry or even the diaconate is very appealing to me, but being twenty-nine, I am too young for the diaconate, so I have a few years to discern. Having a family now would mean that the wages earned would have to be enough for us. As a Catholic couple we are discerning home schooling and trying to find ways where my wife can be home while we have small children. So if it's God's will I will do my best to answer.

At this time, raising a young family is most important to me. I need money to pay my bills and provide for my family. I don't feel the church would provide this. I want my children to know me and I feel that if I spent my time now involved with the church, it would take away time with them. Possibly I might get more involved after they're older and I have more time to myself.

(3) The pay is too low

The comments mentioned not only low pay but low job security. Examples from college students:

It doesn't seem to be a good enough source of prosperity to raise a family.

Given the future of our economy and threat of no social security, it is important that I am able to support myself and have good job security. I would rather volunteer on the side and have a steady paycheck than be worried about living paycheck-to-paycheck.

I wish to be financially secure before considering the possibility of full-time work with the Catholic Church.

To be completely honest, I don't exactly know what encompasses being a lay minister. I just know working for the Church can have low pay, and although I know it will be rewarding in many other aspects, I have always dealt with a fear about security.

From the diocesan sample:

I feel terrible saying this, but to give an honest answer my current lifestyle could not be supported financially.

I have been a witness to the lives of many lay ministers for years now. These people are very dedicated to their work; however, the financial reward would not coincide with my own personal desires. There is entirely too much personal sacrifice to enter full-time lay ministry, especially in terms of being able to live a decent middle-class lifestyle.

The pay would be considerably lower than my current pay, which would mean that my family and I would need to consider other ways of earning possible income.

I am interested a little bit, but have a full-time occupation that I like for now. Given the right circumstances, it could be a great way for me to utilize my gifts and have a very fulfilling career, albeit one that doesn't pay enough at this point to be the sole source of household income.

Whilst lay ministry is essential for the future of the church, there are a multitude of reasons why I prefer to seek work outside the church. As the spouse of a lay minister, I have intimate knowledge of the challenges facing lay ministers. First, it's nearly impossible to earn a livable wage. Likewise, I feel that lay ministers are not offered the respect they deserve. Also, my spouse works long hours, especially in the evening and on weekends. Working nontraditional hours takes away from the time my spouse can spend with family and friends—just so we can barely get by financially.

Meet Anna, a College Student Interested in Lay Ministry

Anna is a senior in a large university, age twenty-one, majoring in international relations and religious studies. She grew up in the Midwest. Now she is president of the Catholic Student Association at the university. She is engaged to be married. Anna is articulate about her motivations and the motivations of other students in the Catholic Center.

For a long time I thought I was called to be a nun. My patron saint that I picked for confirmation is St. Catherine of Sweden. And she's the patron saint of mothers. Abortion is kind of one of the issues I'm really close to. I have a real affinity for life, praying for the unborn and for mothers who are expecting children. And I've had a lot of friends who have struggled with it. So it's been a really close thing to me. So I chose her for my saint. I thought protecting mothers and the unborn was really important. But I looked to her and I looked to Mary and they actually both had a chaste lifestyle, so I always saw myself fitting into that whole thing.

But God didn't really see that for me (laugh). Now I have a fiancé. I have a whole new saint that I pray with now and can appreciate life in a very different way. My fiancé has a different prayer life than I do; he's very nature-oriented and sees God when he's outdoors and doing things.

Interviewer: *In the future there will be many jobs in lay ministry opening up in the Catholic Church. Have you ever thought about that?*

Yeah. Oh, absolutely!

Interviewer: *What would you like to do?*

I love working with youth and I think with my pull to education, I could definitely see myself working for a campus ministry or working for a youth group at a parish. I think youth are really, really important for the future and the progression of the church, and I think it keeps one's faith lively to see children and young people really passionate about the love of Christ. Especially, you know, when Jesus said, let the children come to him, it is children who hold the essence of a lot of what God wants. So I just think that would be a good place for me to keep my own spirituality very healthy, but also to pass on the knowledge and experiences that I've had, which I think are really important, to pass them on to others.

Interviewer: *Do you see lay ministry as more or less equivalent to being a sister? I mean, if you are a married minister as opposed to being a celibate? How are those related?*

Kind of, in a way. There's always the vocation of your job—I mean a vocation as a sacrament, in a sense. They're not entirely separate and they definitely go hand in hand. Like, for example, there could be sisters like the

Little Sisters of the Poor, who may have jobs outside of being a sister. Like being a teacher, or some people do finances or some sisters will help babysit or will cook for the other sisters. So there are different parts that you play within your vocation. And I think in the same way, even though I could teach religion and a sister could teach religion, we have the common vocation of religious education, but we would have different vocations in terms of how we identify with God through the kind of commitment that we face. They're not entirely separate, but there are some areas where you can work, whether you're a sister or a layperson.

Interviewer: *Do you feel that God has called you to minister in this way?*

I do. He calls everyone to minister, but some people more overtly than others.

Interviewer: *How about you?*

Yeah, definitely. I think I'm very overtly called because I'm not ashamed to be identified with the Catholic faith; I have no problems speaking out about what I believe and what I know; I feel very confident in my faith, especially at this point in my life. And I know, some people struggle with that, so they may not be ready for that sort of commitment. And I'm also living in a country that allows me to be expressive and to not fear repercussions as much as other countries. So I feel like I've been given so much that God would really like for me to answer back.

Interviewer: *Have you been around lay ministers in your parish life and elsewhere?*

> Yeah. My parents are still lay ministers—Eucharistic ministers and lectors, and involved. They used to volunteer at my church and in a group called CARE. And they provided anonymous service to parishioners, anything from lawn care to helping an elderly person shower or take their medications on time and watch over them, to babysitting. They provided all these services for free and anonymously and they were all lay ministers.

Interviewer: *This research is mainly about seeing if people are interested in being full-time paid lay ministers. Are you a candidate for that?*

> Yeah.

Interviewer: *Now I want you to think not only about yourself, but also your friends. Guess why some people would be motivated to think about being a regularly salaried lay minister in the future.*

> The people that I see going into that profession would be in it truly because they want to serve God. There's no financial incentive, no status incentive, none of that. I think it's perceived as a very humbling position to work for the Church. So I think that the incentive is 100 percent completely wanting to serve God. And the people that I see doing that are people who are very strong in their faith, who would have no problem identifying quickly as a Catholic and wouldn't mind

putting on a résumé that they served doing something Catholic. Things like that. So I think it has truly to do with serving God. I can't think of any other factor actually that would motivate them.

Interviewer: *Now I'm going to ask about the other side. Why would people not want to do it?*

I think, among my friends, the number one factor why people wouldn't want to is because they don't agree with everything the Catholic Church does, and to affiliate themselves with the Catholic Church there would be one or two points where they'd fall out and they may not want that full title. But I also think other factors would include finances. They feel like working for the Church would not give them a lot of money. I think a lot of people are very concerned about money, especially after graduation. They look for something that pays better rather than maybe something where you can be happier.

But also I don't know how advertised it is. All the services that we're given at the university, like when you have a career day or something, there's no Catholic representation. Catholic Relief Services does have a lot of jobs. But when they advertise, they're very big on saying "You don't have to be Catholic," which is very good, but there's nothing targeting Catholics, saying we need someone committed to Catholicism for this job.

Interviewer: *You said some people didn't want to be identified with the Catholic Church because they didn't agree with everything. Is that a big problem or just a problem for a few people?*

Here at _____ University, it's a huge problem. I serve on a leadership board with eight other Catholics, and these are people who ran for the election, who chose to be identified as a leader in the Catholic Church. And only eight people out of the entire Catholic population! And I can tell you that probably four of them don't agree on the abortion issue; probably four of them don't agree about women not being able to become priests; you definitely have disagreement about birth control; I would say that the vast majority of people say that birth control is okay. I would say that the majority of people accept homosexuality and gay marriages. We have a very liberal campus.

Interviewer: *Is that a problem for you or not?*

It is a problem. It's really hard. It's hard, because those are exactly the people that I would want to be heavily involved in Catholicism, because the more they're involved in the community, the more they can learn from others. They can pray. They can hear the word of God every time. I'm so glad they go. But it's just really hard when they're on the other side of the issue. And it's really hard to be a Catholic in that situation and hear, "Well, your friend _____ doesn't," or "She's still Catholic and she's normal" in terms of what everyone else believes on campus. So it's very difficult. I'm very torn on the issue, because I love those people very much.

Interviewer: *It seems that it would be hard for Catholics to live that way. Wouldn't they have a problem of integrity?*

Yeah. (laugh) It's very difficult. The vast majority of the population that they're around is much more liberal in terms of those touchy issues. When they don't identify with the other people is when, I think, they become fearful that they'll be rejected by other people, that they won't be accepted in their sorority or other groups.

Interviewer: *Some people are unhappy because women are not taken seriously enough by the Catholic leadership. Is that a problem or not?*

No, not at all. Especially, thinking about motherhood as a vocation, when people say, "Why can't a woman consecrate bread as Jesus?" I say, "Well, why can't a man ever have a life within him and conceive of a life?" Both genders have amazing abilities that they have been given by God. When people are saying that women are oppressed or women don't get their voice, they don't understand how beautiful the gifts are that women have. They're devaluing motherhood. They're devaluing women's service. That's what God loves the most, the humblest positions.

3

Interest in Ministry as a Priest, Brother, Sister, or Deacon

Becoming a priest would allow me to live out a calling to service that God has given me through a way that can directly affect the lives of many people in a positive way.

A man in his 30s

The idea of giving myself completely to something is attractive. As a priest I could surrender myself completely. The many small choices and decisions of lay life would be made for me. It would be like being a soldier. I would take orders and obey with all my heart and soul.

A man in his 30s

I am interested in ministry as a sister because I think it is a powerful witness to the world of the greatness of Jesus and how much we all need to be willing to give up for him. I want other people to find the joy of knowing Jesus, and I think that I could use my gifts to share Jesus with others as a sister.

A woman in her 20s

I feel the call deep in my heart, and it is persistent. I know he waits for my yes. I want to give my entire self to him. I see the vows of poverty, chastity, and obedience as beautiful, and I would like to grow closer to Christ through them. The only huge problem is that I know it is my call, and I want to give him my yes so much, but I cannot because I have a lot of debt from the Catholic college I attended, and the orders will not accept people with educational loans.

A woman in her 30s

Table 3.1
Interest in Ministry as a Priest or Vowed Religious
(in percents)

	Student Sample		Diocesan Sample	
	Males	Females	Males	Females
Have you ever seriously considered becoming a priest?				
Yes	48	1	54	3
Have you ever seriously considered becoming a sister or a brother?				
Yes	18	39	30	37
Has anyone ever encouraged you to consider ministry as a priest, brother, or sister?				
Yes	70	33	71	39

A different option for future service is to do ministry as a priest, religious brother, or religious sister. We asked the respondents if they had ever seriously considered these possibilities. The numbers are high. See Table 3.1. Forty-eight percent of the men in the college student sample and 54 percent of those in the diocesan sample said they had once seriously considered becoming a priest. The numbers who have seriously

Table 3.2

Interest in Ministry as a Priest or Vowed Religious at Three Levels of Involvement in Campus Ministry (in percents)

	College Student Sample		
	Officer or leader	Participant	Not involved
Have you ever seriously considered becoming a priest? (men only)			
Yes	56	46	39
Have you ever seriously considered becoming a sister or a brother?			
Yes	43	27	22
Has anyone ever encouraged you to consider ministry as a priest, brother, or sister?			
Yes	61	45	33

considered becoming a brother or sister were lower, but still quite high. Apparently many young Catholics ponder these options at some time in their lives.

Has anyone encouraged these young people to consider ministry as a priest, brother, or sister? The third item in Table 3.1 shows that of the men, the clear majority said yes—70 percent of the college men and 71 percent of the men in the diocesan sample. For the women, about one-third had been encouraged to become a sister—33 percent of the college women and 39 percent of the women in the diocesan sample. There was much more encouragement for the young men than the young women.

Table 3.2 breaks down the college sample according to their level of involvement in the Catholic campus ministry. The rightmost column is a rough approximation of the majority of Catholic college students, because on any campus the majority of Catholics are not active in the Catholic campus ministry.

Table 3.3				
If Anyone Has Ever Encouraged You to Consider Ministry as a Priest or Vowed Religious (in percents; up to three responses coded in any response)				
	College Sample		Diocesan Sample	
	Men	Women	Men	Women
Number of cases:	(113)	(56)	(107)	(49)
Priest	62	34	78	43
Parent or grandparent	30	20	36	53
Friend	30	18	36	35
Teacher	18	18	21	27
Other relative	11	4	5	12
Parishioner	7	7	8	4
Nun or sister	4	16	1	47
Other	9	7	9	12

Even in this third column, the number of persons who have once seriously considered becoming a priest, brother, or sister is fairly high—at least 22 percent.

We asked a question to everyone: "If anyone has ever encouraged you to consider ministry as a priest, who (parent, priest, teacher, etc.)?" The responses are summarized in Table 3.3. This question was written with men respondents in mind, but in the online survey both men and women could answer it. We analyzed the responses given by both genders. For the men in both samples, priests were by far the most important source of encouragement. Not many women responded to the question (only fifty-six in the college sample and forty-nine in the diocesan sample), but their sources of encouragement were diverse.

We wanted to know how seriously these persons had considered ministry in the priesthood or religious life. To measure

Table 3.4

What Steps Have the Interested Persons Taken?

(in percents)

If you have considered becoming either a priest, sister or brother, have you taken any of the following steps to explore this form of ministry? (check all that apply; percentages of anyone saying "yes" to one of the first two questions)

	Student Sample		Diocesan Sample	
	Males	Females	Males	Females
Spoke to friends about it	79	56	79	71
Spoke to parents or other relatives	62	43	51	61
Spoke to a priest, religious, or lay minister	81	46	81	62
Spoke to a career counselor	6	1	9	6
Gathered printed information	29	24	48	45
Looked online for information	31	36	44	47
Asked for information from a vocation director	24	14	49	30

this, we asked, had they been interested enough to take any action? For most, yes. Table 3.4 tells us that the vast majority had spoken to friends, priests, religious, or lay ministers about it. Over half had spoken with parents or other relatives. Generally, the persons in the diocesan sample had taken more of these steps than the college students, especially speaking to friends, relatives, priests, and religious.

What Encourages or Discourages a Call to Ministry in the Priesthood or Religious Life?

Table 3.5 assesses the factors encouraging and discouraging interest in these vocations. The top half shows the encouragers, listed in descending order. The main ones are "it is a response

Table 3.5

Reasons For and Against Interest in Ministry
as a Priest or Vowed Religious (in percents)

Here are reasons sometimes given for interest in becoming a priest, sister, or brother. Whether or not you are personally interested, how important would each be to you? (check all that apply)

	Student Sample		Diocesan Sample	
	Males	Females	Males	Females
It is a response to God's call	85	85	89	90
It is an opportunity to help other people	74	81	82	82
It is an opportunity to preach God's Word	63	59	72	61
It utilizes my gifts and talents	49	58	62	64
It is an opportunity to provide the Sacraments	49	37	58	44
It will help me get to heaven	24	25	30	35

Here are reasons sometimes given for not becoming a priest, sister, or brother. How influential would each be in discouraging you, whether or not you are personally interested? (check all that apply)

	Student Sample		Diocesan Sample	
	Males	Females	Males	Females
I have a different career in mind	71	70	46	52
Not allowed to marry	60	68	44	59
Too many rules and regulations	20	26	21	23
A lifelong commitment is required	30	32	19	26
People in these vocations are often lonely	16	17	15	18
Church structures are too undemocratic	10	17	14	20
Church structures are too dominated by men	9	27	10	33
I am not spiritual enough	13	17	9	16
A lack of privacy	5	10	5	13
This vocation is not highly respected	1	3	3	7
I know too little about it to be interested	7	12	3	10

to God's call" and "it is an opportunity to help other people." These two were the main motivations for both samples.

The bottom of Table 3.5 shows the discouraging factors. Two of them are far ahead of all the others: "I have a different career in mind" and "Not allowed to marry." Two other discouragers are moderately important, but less than the first two: "Too many rules and regulations" and "A lifelong commitment is required."

Are these encouragers and discouragers different for active versus nonactive Catholics? In the student sample we compared the persons active or not active in campus ministry. The ranking of factors was the same for active and nonactive Catholics, while the level of encouragement reported by the active Catholics was higher. Possibly most interesting was the finding that 20 percent of the noninvolved students said "I know too little about it to be interested," and an additional 26 percent thought they were not spiritual enough to consider an ordained or vowed vocation. Apparently, for many Catholic college students, this option was never strongly in their minds.

How many persons are seriously considering these options now? We should expect that the numbers will be lower than the numbers who have considered the options at some point or other in their past. We can estimate the percentages interested now from an open-ended question in the survey which asked, "In your own words, why are you interested or uninterested in ministry as a priest, brother, or sister?" Table 3.6 summarizes the number of answers indicating interest or disinterest in these vocations now. Our samples had twenty-four college

Table 3.6

Summary of Persons Now Interested in Becoming a Priest, Brother, or Sister (number of cases)

	College Sample		Diocesan Sample	
	Men	Women	Men	Women
No. of persons responding:	(131)	(187)	(126)	(219)
Open-Ended Responses about Being Interested or Uninterested Now				
Number interested now	24	14	13	22
Number undecided now or who wrote in uncodable comments	11	14	18	10
Number not interested now	96	159	95	87

men, fourteen college women, thirteen older men, and twenty-two older women seriously interested now.

Here is important information, indicating how many of our sample respondents are currently considering priesthood or vowed religious life. These lists of college students compiled by campus ministers and lists of young adults compiled by diocesan offices contain very fruitful prospects for future interest in priesthood or religious life. This should not be surprising, since the people on these lists are known to be active in church life and serious about their faith.

How many of these people can we reasonably expect will enter later? Not many. Nationwide data tells us that the total number doing so each year in the United States is low. We tried to make estimates based on available statistics. Nationwide data on seminary enrollments suggests that about 750 men enter seminaries at the theology level each year. (The number of ordinations each year was about 450 in 2006–2007 because some seminarians drop out before ordination; see CARA 2007.) The total number of Catholic men age twenty-five to twenty-nine in the United States was about 2,480,000 in 2006, based on census data. Thus, if 750 of them enter seminary each year, it is about .0003 of all the Catholic men in that age bracket. The rate of men entering the seminary is very low.

If we conduct a thought experiment and estimate that the men in our samples are thirty times more likely to enter seminary as a random sample of Catholic men of this age, the seminary-goers in our sample would still be only .009, or 0.9 percent of the sample. Let us round this up to one percent, a somewhat optimistic estimate. Thus we guess that one percent of our sample will actually attend seminary in the future; it seems a reasonable estimate. The rest will choose other careers.

We cannot make an analogous estimate for women entering into vowed religious communities because we lack data on the number entering each year. From available information, the rate of entering religious life is lower for women than for men.

Reasons Given by Respondents for Their Interest or Lack of Interest

We have seen that large proportions of Catholic youth seriously consider ministering as a priest or vowed religious at some time in their lives, yet most change their minds later. Why? We asked all the respondents to tell us in their own words why they are now interested or uninterested in ministry as a priest, brother, or sister. We divided the samples into persons interested and uninterested, then categorized the responses of each group. See Tables 3.7 and 3.8.

Table 3.7

Interested Persons: Why Interested in Becoming a Priest, Brother, or Sister? (in percents; up to two codes in any response)

	College Sample		Diocesan Sample	
	Men	Women	Men	Women
Number of responses:	**(24)**	**(14)**	**(13)**	**(22)**
I feel called; I wish to follow God	42	7	62	14
To preach God's Word; to teach about God; to save souls	33	14	31	14
To serve God; to do God's will	17	14	38	36
To be holy; to be closer to God; to give my whole self	13	64	15	68
To help people	8	29	8	18
My talents and skills fit these roles	8	7	8	0
To administer the blessed sacraments	4	0	8	0

Table 3.7 gives the responses of persons currently interested in priesthood or religious life. There were twenty-four men and fourteen women in the college sample, thirteen men and twenty-two women in the diocesan sample. We coded up to two ideas in each of their responses, shown in the table in descending order.

The men wrote, above all, of a feeling of being called. In addition they wrote of their desire to preach God's Word, to teach about God, to save souls, and to serve God. The women gave somewhat different responses, emphasizing their desire to be holy, to be closer to God, and to give their whole selves. Also, some told of their desire to serve God and to help people.

What holds other Catholics back from following these paths? Table 3.8 summarizes the reasons the people gave. The

Table 3.8

Uninterested Persons: Why Uninterested in Becoming a Priest, Brother, or Sister?

(in percents; up to two codes in any response)

	College Sample		Diocesan Sample	
	Men	Women	Men	Women
Number of responses:	(96)	(159)	(95)	(187)
I prefer to marry; to have a family	46	54	65	71
I prefer another career; in another career	29	16	13	4
I do not feel called	10	10	7	11
I am not a good enough person; not enough faith or education	8	12	1	3
Too confining; too lonely; too scary	4	6	0	0
I disagree with the Church positions on some issues	3	2	8	5
My gifts and talents lie elsewhere	2	5	3	2
The Church is too male-dominated; not enough respect for women	0	5	2	9
I know too little about it to be interested	2	2	0	0

most important discourager, by far, is these people's desire to marry and have a family. It is a bit stronger for the women than for the men, but for both genders it is clearly the number-one discourager.

The second most important discourager is that the respondents have already chosen other careers, a more important factor for the men than for the women. This information raises another question: why had they chosen the other careers? What was the reason? We return to this topic below.

Other important discouragers were (1) the person did not feel called, and (2) the person did not feel he or she was a good enough person in faith or education. In addition, among the women, 5 percent of the college women and 9 percent of the older women said they felt the Church was too male-dominated and had too little respect for women.

Questions Specific to Men

We put three additional questions to men, shown in Table 3.9. First, would they be seriously interested in becoming an ordained priest if celibacy were not required? Twenty percent of the college men and 27 percent of the older men said yes. These findings need to be compared with the percent seriously interested in becoming a priest now. As Table 3.6 showed us, the numbers currently interested in priesthood or religious life were (college men and women) 18 percent, 7 percent, and (noncollege men and women) 10 percent and 10 percent, respectively, of the total number of respondents.

We see that the number of men entering the priesthood would increase if celibacy was not required, but we cannot say by how much. Among the college men, the increase would be modest, but among the older men the number interested would double or triple.

What if priesthood could be for a limited period of time, maybe five or ten years, instead of lifelong? As the second item in Table 3.9 shows, interest would increase among the men in the diocesan sample, but not by as much. (For college men, the 18 percent in Table 3.9 is similar to the 18 percent based on Table 3.6; for older men, the 15 percent in Table 3.9 is a bit higher than the 10 percent based on Table 3.6.)

How about the men's interest in becoming a permanent deacon? Very few are interested now, but about half of each

Table 3.9

Men's Attitudes About Vocations (in percents)

(men only:)	Student Sample	Diocesan Sample
Would you be seriously interested in becoming an ordained priest if celibacy were not required?		
Yes	20	27
No	37	44
Don't know	44	29
Would you be seriously interested in becoming an ordained priest if you could sign up for a limited time period, renewable, for maybe 5 or 10 years?		
Yes	18	15
No	45	57
Don't know	37	28
Would you be seriously interested in becoming a permanent deacon at some time?		
Yes, soon	2	10
Not soon, but maybe later	46	54
No	23	21
Don't know	28	15

sample would maybe be interested later. Put simply: our samples contain a large pool of men who are future candidates for the diaconate. We need to explain that Church rules prohibit a man from marrying after becoming a permanent deacon. Thus, if a young man becomes a deacon he cannot marry at any time later. The young men we interviewed pointed this out as a reason for delaying becoming a permanent deacon until later, or much later, so as to keep the marriage option open.

Are the numbers of men potentially interested in the priesthood or diaconate in Table 3.9 dependent on levels of involvement in campus ministry? We compared the involved and noninvolved and found that the differences were modest. The main difference was that the college men active in campus

Table 3.10
Women's Attitudes (in percents)

(women only:)	Student Sample	Diocesan Sample
If women could be ordained, would you be interested in becoming a priest?		
Yes	13	10
No	65	71
Don't know	22	19
If the permanent diaconate becomes available to women, would you be seriously interested?		
Yes, soon	4	7
Not soon, but maybe later	25	22
No	43	52
Don't know	28	19

ministry programs were much more interested in the diaconate than the noninvolved men.

Questions Specific to Women

We put two questions to the women. See Table 3.10. First, "If women could be ordained, would you be interested in becoming a priest?" Among the college women, 13 percent said yes and 87 percent said no or don't know. Among the women in the diocesan sample, 10 percent said yes and 90 percent said no or don't know.

Second, "If the permanent diaconate becomes available to women, would you be seriously interested?" As was the case with the men, not many would be interested now, but some would maybe be interested later—25 percent of the college women and 22 percent of the women in the diocesan sample. These two questions give the estimates of the number of women candidates for the priesthood and diaconate, if these vocations ever became open to women in the future.

As with the men students, we divided the women students into three levels of involvement with campus ministry, to see if the involved were different from the noninvolved. As expected, the women most active in campus ministry were more interested than the others in becoming a priest or a permanent deacon in the future, if these possibilities become available.

Examples of Written-in Reasons for Interest in Priesthood or Religious Life

Our survey gathered good information on factors encouraging or discouraging ministry as a priest or vowed religious. We summarized them in Table 3.7, and here we display some typical responses. Three factors were the most common and powerful: (1) I feel called, or I wish to follow God; (2) To preach God's Word; to teach about God; to save souls; to serve God; and (3) To be holy or to be closer to God. The examples below convey the flavor of the responses. As one can see, they are heartfelt and thoughtful.

(1) I feel called, or I wish to follow God

From men, both students and older persons:

> *Becoming a priest would allow me to live out a calling to service that God has given me through a way that can directly affect the lives of many people in a positive way.*

> *I am very interested in being a priest and have done much research, especially into that of being an Augustinian Canon. I feel that this way of life would be the best answer to God's call to the ministry [for me]. I am interested because there is a shortage of priests and because*

I feel that God is calling me to be holy and to serve him in this way.

It is an answer to a calling that I may have, and it would be an amazing thing to help others find their faith and to help them in their times of need.

A desire to serve God and bring his love to the world, and a feeling of being called.

I am interested in ministry as a priest because I feel a calling from God. I feel as though God has planned this for me.

From women, both students and older persons:

I am interested because it could be what God wants me to do.

My understanding of any vocational calling is that it is not anything like a "career move," but a calling from almighty God. Your vocation is your "yellow brick road to sanctity," and it lies at the intersection of your deepest desires, your gifts and talents, and the needs of your community.

(2) To preach God's Word; to teach about God; to save souls; to serve God

From men:

It would allow me to teach Christ's words to others.

My interest in becoming a priest is rooted in the idea that I would like my life to do God's will as much as possible.

We are called to serve and spread the light of Christ to others. Therefore if this is the best way to utilize my talents, it is what I should be doing.

From women:

If I felt the call to be a sister I would think it an amazing privilege no one is worthy of, but nonetheless serves to glorify God and build his Church. To be consecrated for Christ—to be set aside for him—sets me in awe. You are called to live the Gospel perfectly, you are called to die to yourself, you are called to give yourself entirely to our Lord Jesus Christ. Truly Christ gives you everything in this very special call. If called, heck yes, I am interested, knowing that it would be his grace that would enable such a life lived in love for him, his people, and Church.

I am interested because then I could focus on God without as much business from other people and work. My career would be always serving him in an unforgettable way; can't push it aside.

I would be interested in becoming a sister because of the feeling of having a purpose in life—something greater than making money.

To me a religious vocation is a vocation to love, as a witness to God's love and conduit of God's love, as you

*interact with others or as you pray for them. My expe-
rience of God's love and grace compels me to desire
to give more, to love more, to search for more, every
moment drawing closer to my goal of union with Christ in
heaven. Over the past two years of prayer and discernment I have come to desire to serve Christ and the Church
in poverty, chastity, and obedience to give him glory and
save souls.*

(3) To be holy or to be closer to God

From men:

*It's not about ministry, according to the understanding of
this survey. It's about God's deeply personal invitation to
an individual to seek him, to seek his face and to become
like unto Him, to resemble Him more closely in his image
and likeness. Everything else is accidental, circumstantial—
work, apostolates, spouse, children, everything. I am interested in seeking the One who made me. Trinity of Persons
in ontological unity. When I seek him earnestly, he will
show me how to run to himself all the more.*

*It's an invitation from Christ that is offered to me that
seems like it may fulfill who I REALLY am deep down. I'll
give it a try.*

From women:

*I find the simplicity of religious life extremely compel-
ling, and I see great grace that comes from the sacrifice
involved in making such a commitment.*

I think it is a great way to grow in devotion to God and help others.

I would be very interested in a ministry as a consecrated hermit, virgin, or secular institute member because I want to give my life for Jesus through our Blessed Mother. I am interested in solitary life because I can make my own work and prayer schedule.

The world, and even some in the church, seem to emphasize what someone gives up to be religious, rather than what one gains. Rather than simply "not being able to be married," the accent must instead lie on the fact that religious give themselves totally to Christ. And in some mysterious mystical way, they receive him in a way that likely can only be understood by those who have experienced it for themselves. They are a reminder to the whole church that this world is not our home, that we are all destined for the eternal marriage feast of the Lamb. They anticipate and live out on earth what all human persons saved by God's grace will experience for all eternity—total union with God.

The religious life is a beautiful witness in today's world and much needed. I have always had great respect for those who consecrate their lives to God in this way. It would be an amazing challenge, and I am drawn to a life that allows one to spend so much time in prayer. I also love the outward radical witness of the priest's clerics and a sister's habit. It makes me happy to see them wearing them in public.

Examples of Written-in Reasons for Disinterest in Ministry as Priest or Religious

As we saw in Table 3.8, there are four main impediments. One is the largest by far: not allowed to marry. The other three are (2) I prefer another career; (3) I do not feel called; and (4) I am not a good enough person—not enough faith or education. Here are examples of what the respondents wrote, beginning with the question of marriage.

(1) I prefer to marry and to have a family

From men:

> I don't want to become a priest, because I BADLY want a wife and children.

> I am a little interested in becoming a priest because it provides a great calling for God and the church. I just sometimes doubt I can make a lifelong commitment and not be lonely without family.

> I have been in a relationship with the same person for almost three years now, and I have trouble imagining that God would keep us together this long only to have us break up. Not being able to marry is a big deal for me.

> I am uninterested because of the loneliness accompanied by the priesthood. If priests were allowed to get married, or if I am not married by a certain age (let's say forty), then I will think about it.

The only impediment is that I like women too much. I do not think I could serve as a priest with that in mind.

I was interested in the priesthood and also in marriage. My girlfriend at the time and I prayed together, offering my services either way, and I felt comfortable pursuing marriage. We still feel "approved" in our decision to marry.

Since just before my marriage I have always pondered the priesthood or becoming a brother. A couple of priests even approached me at retreats before noticing my wedding band. I have even considered converting to Greek Orthodox, but it is just not the same. It is the cross I bear.

From women:

Number one: I want to have a family. This is why I have never considered being a sister.

As a sister, I would be unable to get married. In addition, I do not agree with some of the positions that the Catholic Church takes on various social issues.

At this time I am uninterested in ministry as a sister because I think I would really like to have the love and bond that comes along with marriage. I am also looking forward to having children. These feelings may change in the future, but for now this is why I am not interested in becoming a sister.

I have given fair consideration to being a sister when I've heard people talk about it, but I feel as if I am meant to marry and have a family. I pray about what God really wants me to do, and feel more strongly pulled in the direction of married life. I have always wanted to have children and can still see myself having a close relationship with God as a mother and wife.

I want to get married and have children and follow my vocation by raising them to be good Catholics growing up in a safe Catholic home.

(2) I prefer another career

From men:

I was interested when I was much younger in grade school, but eventually concluded that my particular gifts were geared towards another field—architecture—and that I wasn't necessarily being called by God just because my priest had asked if I ever thought about it.

It is God's will in my life to be working with Marriott. He has led me there every step of the way, therefore it is a response to God's call. Perhaps in the future I'll be called to enter the seminary.

I think my talents are better used elsewhere. Specifically, God blessed me with an ability to formulate logical arguments, manipulate symbols, and wrap my mind around complex mathematical structures, so my calling is to be a scientist.

I'm not interested in becoming a priest because I would rather work in the field of international relations. I feel this field provides a great avenue to work for social justice.

From women:

It is not my calling, not the right thing for me. I am pursuing a career in education and that's what I'm good at. Also I wouldn't want to have all the rules and not get married.

I'm a full-time resident of ophthalmology.

I am a woman and therefore would feel disrespected by the Church and the community if I chose a path like that. The Church's structure has an inherently inferior position for women, and I could never commit my life to such standards. I can contribute much more to society when I'm not bound by the Church's sexist restrictions, as I am now doing as an attorney helping less fortunate people.

I really want to be a wife and have a career. I don't want to give up my chance of writing and reporting.

(3) I do not feel called
From men:

I have seen the passion and faithfulness of the priests at my Newman Center, and it has helped me see the passion and strength of the Church. At this time, I do not believe that I am called to the priesthood, so I look to serve the Church in other ways.

If I am serious about living my life for God, I should at least consider priestly ministry. I do not think it is my calling, however.

Too much of a commitment, and I don't feel like that is my calling.

I have considered the priestly vocation, but I do not think that it is what God is calling me to. There are a few things. I am attracted to the idea of celebrating the sacraments. At the same time, it seems like priests in parish ministry are forced to tolerate the liturgical abuses fostered by their predecessors for pastoral reasons. The thought of preaching the gospel is attractive. I am very attached to the classical Roman Rite. Most bishops wrongly have a negative impression of this ritual, overlooking the beauty present in it. There are very few bishops in America who ordain men interested in this ritual. This is especially the case in my own diocese. Also I was dissuaded from the priesthood by the politics; I dislike the way orthodox and traditional priests are persecuted by their brother priests.

From women:

I feel like God would have called on me already if he wanted me to become a sister.

I would love to be married to Christ and see this as a very important and respectable profession. However, I feel God has called me to follow a different path.

I entered the convent about seven years ago but was there only for three weeks. I know a lot of the problem was missing my family, but I truly think I don't have a vocation to the religious life. If God calls me there I'll answer, but I'm pretty sure I'm where he wants me to be right now.

(4) I am not a good enough person—not enough faith or education

From men:

I have actually thought seriously about this a number of times. I have wondered if God is calling me to do this. However I am not quite sure, and I feel that I am not a good enough person to be such an agent of God.

Although I respect and admire the priesthood, I do not feel I have the discipline nor the calling to do so myself.

I feel I am not the ideal candidate to take on such a position. I need to grow deeper in my faith before such a vocation can be considered.

I've always seen myself to be more faithful than my friends and others around me, but not so much so to consider life as a priest or brother.

From women:

I am not very interested in ministry as a sister because I feel called to other work. I also don't feel that I know enough and have enough faith to fulfill such a role.

I am uninterested because I am not devoted enough. I do not believe everything that the Catholic Church says.

I have not become a faithful enough Christian to preach God's teachings. I am too much of a sinner.

It would be a great way to help people and utilize my gifts at the same time. I would love to do it but the total spiritual commitment scares me.

I have been interested in becoming a sister because I see it as a way of helping people, and a spiritual life is attractive. But I don't believe that I could become a sister simply because I believe God wants me to marry and because frankly I am interested too much in money.

Ben, a Man with a History of Discerning the Priesthood and Diaconate

Ben is a Catholic school teacher in the Midwest and a graduate student earning a masters degree in English. He is twenty-five years old, engaged to be married soon. Several years ago he spent a year as a seminarian, then left, but today he still desires to do ministry, probably as a lay minister, teacher, or deacon. The interviewer asked if he would be interested in full-time lay ministry:

When I was really discerning religious life, I intentionally said that being a lay minister is not an option, because I had some desires in my heart for religious life. I didn't just want to create a false "middle" life, you know, like that some of those desires will be fulfilled by being involved in the church, but by not taking the leap into ordained ministry. So for a while I just sort of had to say "Not an option," because I had to consider the priesthood thing.

But now that we have sort of moved past that (laugh) I think I really would. I mean, now I'm on a track to teach and to write, which is something I have desires for. But if the opportunity presented itself, I think I would certainly consider that [lay ministry]. I think I still sometime may need to discern even the permanent diaconate.

I definitely have a desire to be involved in the life of the church, whether that's just on a volunteer basis or whether it's as an employee. And I think my brief time in the seminary—then you're sort of looking from the perspective of the clergy—and just in my brief moments having that vantage point, I think it helped me see even more just how important strong lay leadership is and how it's needed. And so whether it becomes something more formal or whether it's just somehow being a lay leader in the parish on a strictly volunteer basis, it's definitely something I want to be involved in.

Interviewer: *Do you feel that God has ever called you to ministry?*

Yes. (long pause) That's hard to articulate. I guess what I would say is that many of the desires that took me to seminary haven't gone away. I mean, it's still a part of my person, you know. So whether or not that was my calling, God has placed those desires in my heart.

But obviously the important thing to me right now is my classwork, my schoolwork, getting married, really building a foundation for that life together. And then once that's in place, then I think I'll be more open to that possibility.

Interviewer: *If one day you consider this kind of ministry, what kind of employment might you be interested in?*

Not teaching CCD, that is, education for church children. I love kids, but I'm not sure that I have the patience for it, or the gifts for it. I think I'd certainly be interested in adult ed. If my life takes me in such a way that I become a professor at a university, I'd sure be interested in helping out at a Newman Center. I mean, I would love to somehow be involved in importing some of my undergraduate Newman Center experience at _____ University into another Newman Center. Counseling? I think it is something I could be good at. I've been told I'm a good listener by everyone except my fiancée. (laugh) And I think I can be attentive to other people, and I have some desires for that.

I mean, I want to be involved in the whole life of the church, maybe by some participation in liturgy. Obviously, if I were to discern the diaconate, I think one of the pulls would be the pulpit. Preaching. But probably the two main things would be adult education and counseling.

Interviewer: *What would be your main motivation in being interested?*

Well, that's an excellent question. I need to be cautious that I'm not just doing it for myself. It's not just like this is something I need or I want. I think I need to start thinking in terms of my own immediate family unit—which is still a rather new idea—and what's best for us. In addition to that, I think I need to be in prayer and commune with God enough to really listen to what he wants too.

Interviewer: Would you be interested in any part-time position in ministry?

Yeah, that sounds quite nice. I need to make some money! (laugh) That would be ideal. I think the opportunity would just have to present itself, but I certainly wouldn't rule it out.

Interviewer: Can you talk a little bit about when you were considering ministry as a priest?

I think my experience was that of a typical collegian. In part it was just the question that faces every collegian: What am I doing with my life? What is my life going to look like? And in my diocese, they do a great job of trying to remind kids from a young age on up that the priesthood is an option; it's a possibility; it's a great life! And because of the great need for the religious vocations, there's a movement to remind children of that, especially children who are no longer necessarily getting that reminder in the home. Because like for my parents, it was just not on their radar. It was just not thought of.

But it was just like an eye-opening in college. "This is a possibility. People do this! People enjoy it, you know. People are happy doing this!" It was quite a *revelation, and obviously the dynamic life of both male and female religious at ____ University was an inspiration. There were three or four, and I should say they offered a witness to religious life. Young and energetic, and you just visibly saw how that flowered from their own spiritual life and their own ministry. They all loved what they did, and they all did it well. So I think that was an influence.*

Interviewer: *Here's a theoretical question. Would you be more interested in still becoming a priest if priests could marry?*

You know, that's a difficult question. (thinks) Part of me says yes, that if priests could marry, then it might still be on my radar. But it would be fraught with many questions, I mean, what kind of life would that be? I mean, just such a commitment to the people of God and such a commitment to your spouse and kids. I think to do that would be difficult. And in addition to just the practicalities of it, I think I see more than practical wisdom in a celibate clergy. I see so many fruits in someone who lives celibacy for the kingdom. Having really experienced it as it is, with mandatory celibacy, I'm not hoping that the church will change on this. It's a radical way of life; it's a way of life for the few! Obviously, most of us are going to be lay people, and that's okay.

So I'm not leading a charge for change. I like it the way it is. But if the discipline was removed, I would consider the priesthood, I guess.

Interviewer: *In your own personal discernment, was the marriage question a huge part of your discernment?*

> It was, for sure. I mean, in the simplest terms, it was really a question of whether or not I needed a companion, just for my own journey. In all seriousness, I think that at the heart of my discernment was whether or not I could live this beautiful radical priestly life on my own—of course, God included. Or whether it was sort of done with a helpmate. And in the end I decided that a helpmate was necessary. And so, once you make that determination, it's easy. I'm not like "I really wish I can combine the two."

Interviewer: *What if priests could sign up for a term of ministry for ten or fifteen years and then have an option to stop?*

> I don't like the assumption in that question. What makes priesthood appealing is the theological understanding that the priest carries an eternal indelible mark. A priest is a priest forever. It isn't just a career or job. I don't think you're going to find young people who are like, "Oh, you presented this to me as a wonderful employment opportunity. I'm going to sign on the dotted line." I think the church would be better served by a better theological understanding of priesthood, which is that it is a lifetime commitment and beyond that. That the mark on the soul of the priest remains into eternity. We're not dealing just with a short-time career here or a 25-to-65 career. This is something bigger. And just in my own experience,

when people try to sell it as like "This is a great job," you know, that was repulsive.

Interviewer: *Would you be interested in possibly becoming a deacon?*

I think that will just depend on the future. It's hard to know, but I certainly want to leave that door open for the present time.

Ben is unusual in that he spent a year in a seminary, but he is not unusual in that he feels called to minister and is searching for a job that will enable him to use his gifts in ministry.

4

The Future of Priests and Lay Ministers

Many young adult Catholics see their own possible ministry in the context of future Catholic life, especially life in parishes. What kind of parish life would they like to see? What role do they see for lay ministry in the future? What kind of priests? In our surveys we asked several questions. See Table 4.1.

The first item asks for agreement or disagreement on the statement that the Catholic Church needs to move faster in empowering lay persons in ministry. Fifty percent to sixty percent agreed.

Do priests have the same opinion? This same question was asked in a 2001 survey of a random sample of Catholic priests, and 73 percent of the priests (70 percent of the diocesan priests and 79 percent of the religious priests) agreed (Hoge and Wenger 2003, 51). Older priests agreed much more than younger priests in 2001; the highest agreement was among priests fifty-six to sixty-five years old (86 percent), and lowest agreement was among priests thirty-five or younger (54 percent). Put simply, older priests see a growth in lay ministers as more urgent than do younger priests. The people in our samples are similar to young priests today and have some mixed feelings about the growth in lay ministries.

The second item in Table 4.1 states that ordination confers on the priest a new status or a permanent character, making

Table 4.1

Attitudes on Lay Ministry and Priesthood (in percents)

	Student Sample		Diocesan Sample	
	Males	Females	Males	Females

Do you agree or disagree with the following statement: The Catholic Church needs to move faster in empowering lay persons in ministry.

	Student Sample		Diocesan Sample	
Strongly or somewhat agree	52	54	59	61

Do you agree or disagree: Ordination confers on the priest a new status or a permanent character which makes him essentially different from the laity within the church.

Strongly or somewhat agree	63	56	76	69

Here are two descriptions of priests. Which would you prefer to see in your parish? Choose one.

I prefer a priest who emphasizes the powers of priesthood due to ordination.	22	8	24	17
I prefer a priest who emphasizes the empowerment of lay leadership.	13	20	18	24
Both equally	53	49	49	46
Don't know	12	23	10	12

him essentially different from the laity. Between fifty-six percent and 76 percent of our samples agreed, and men agreed more than women. This statement was also included in the 2001 survey of American priests. In that survey 77 percent of the priests agreed (83 percent of the diocesan priests, 64 percent of the religious). Younger priests agreed much more than older priests.

In other words, diocesan priests tended to hold to a more ontological understanding of the priesthood than the respondents in our samples, and younger diocesan priests had a much stronger attitude than our samples.

This same statement was included in a 2002 survey of lay ministers (Hoge and Wenger 2003, 128). They put slightly less emphasis on ontological differences than the priests did; 69 percent agreed with the statement, compared with 77 percent of the priests. The lay ministers varied slightly by age, with younger persons stressing ontological differences a bit more than the older ones. The lay ministers, in short, held a spectrum of attitudes similar to the respondents in our diocesan survey.

Are college students highly involved in campus ministry different on these topics than the less active? Yes. The leaders of campus ministries expressed more agreement with both statements than other students. The strongest pattern was on the second question about whether ordination confers on the priest a new status or character. Sixty-eight percent of the campus ministry leaders agreed, compared with 48 percent of the least involved. This indicates that campus ministry activists are disproportionately more supportive of existing ecclesiology and existing Church structures.

Preferred Type of Priests

The third question in Table 4.1 asks the respondents to select one of four responses regarding the type of priests they would like to see in their parish. The first two responses were crafted to measure the "cultic" and the "servant leader" models of the priesthood, the first of which emphasizes the separateness of priests from laity and the special powers of the priesthood, and the second of which emphasizes collaboration with laity and the empowerment of lay leadership. Our respondents did not express a strong preference for one or the other. The only pattern in the data was that men, both students and alumni in the diocesan sample, moderately preferred the cultic model, while women students and alumni preferred the servant-leader model.

The most telling pattern in the responses was that well over half of the people had no preference or opinion, suggesting that the issue of different priestly models was unclear or unimportant to them. There could be many reasons for this lack of preference, but the data does not provide those reasons.

Attitudes about Future Priests and Parish Leadership

Our personal interviews included discussion of priests, lay ministers, and parish leadership. A general theme in the interviews was that the people hoped for accessible, collaborative priests and a greater voice for laity. Here are examples.

Anna, whom we met in Chapter 2, talked about what kind of priests Catholics really need:

> I think a key factor is just thinking in terms of a shepherd; that we really need someone to guide us. But at the same time, to be very patient and very gentle, because I think there are a lot of people who desire parts of Catholicism but need a lot of help. And the fire and brimstone doesn't go over very well today.
>
> I think people need someone who listens and gives time, but then guides. He doesn't just listen and say "Okay, well, that's where you stand," but will see where

people are coming from and see that there are genuine problems within society; that there are some things that people have grown up with; maybe, through no fault of their own, maybe through complete fault of their own, have been led astray and really need some guiding in the right direction back. I think that's really important in a priest.

Interviewer: *So, in short, what type of priest do we need?*

A good shepherd, with patience.

Interviewer: *There's some discussion that priests are a little bit too set apart and do not mix enough. Is that a problem or not?*

I don't think priests are set apart; I think that they don't have the time. Just from my own experience, we have a priest who's serving several parishes. So any extra time that he has, has to be spent somewhere else or at another ministry or driving to the next mass or confession. And it's no fault of his own, but there's simply not enough priests in this world, and they're spread so thin.

I think that the job of a priest, if just one man or a few men were in a parish, would be just fine. They would have enough time to do all things sacramental as well as to do everything else: to attend outings with the church group; you have a barbeque outside; to just sit in his office to wait for people to come by. Whatever it may be. But I just think that it's impossible with the shortage of priests.

Interviewer: *When you see priests, do you see them as something apart from other people, basically different?*

I see priests pretty much as the same. I've seen enough come to our Catholic game night or who will just hang out with us on a weekend or will go to dinner with us, or whatever. They're just normal people! Their job is different from mine, but I wouldn't see, outside of the Mass and other sacraments, that he has abilities that I don't have. God won't judge him any differently.

Interviewer: *Do you think that lay ministers will have the difficulty that priests pull rank on them, and say "Look, I'm a priest." Have you heard of that or not?*

No. If anything, I think it would be the other way around, because I think he would say, "I'm a lay minister. I represent the voice of the people. We want change." No, it's not a problem.

Ben, whom we met in Chapter 3, had this to say about his hope for future priests:

It seems to me that holiness is foremost, because everything else can flow out of it. I mean, there's a million important things. There's important people skills; there's important administrative skills. But if their personal interior life isn't at the heart of it, then if they're an introvert and not in a deep relationship with Christ and are wanting to share that with others, then they won't make as much an effort to go out of themselves and be a people person. Or they won't be as concerned with the finances. I mean, at the heart of it has to be a relationship with Christ in a deep way, and everything else flows from that.

Interviewer: *Do you believe that a priest should collaborate with the laity in their ministry?*

Absolutely! Period.

Here are more illustrative quotes from our interviews. A twenty-eight-year-old man talked about the qualities of priests:

Um . . . I would really like to see someone that has shared the same life experiences as I did. Growing up, I never really looked at a priest as being like me at all. He was always, like OK, they always knew they would become priests. They didn't drink in high school, they didn't have girlfriends, that type of thing—and so we always kind of looked at them as being a different breed. Even if it wasn't true, that was kind of the demeanor that I got from them. And so to me, never did I feel that a priest was very approachable for everyday problems. And so I think there should be someone where you can look at the person and say, "You know, I know that this person kind of has gone through this. I'm going to go to them and seek their advice, or seek their counsel." So if I had to choose one quality, it would be that—a feeling of understanding, or similarity.

Interviewer: *It would seem to follow that if you had a choice of having a celibate priest or a married priest in your parish, you might prefer the married.*

> Oh, absolutely, without a doubt! When I went through Pre-Cana to get married, I had heard stories of priests doing it, and what we did was, we had an older couple in our parish who had been married a really long time. We went over to their house and they would cook us breakfast, and we'd just kind of talk about married life. And that was fantastic! It makes no sense to get marriage advice from a priest.

Interviewer: *Among priests there are different theologies. One theology says they should be set apart and another that the priests should be closer to the laity and more collaborative. Which would serve the Church more?*

> Oh, I think way more being a part of the community. The whole idea of Church is that it should be an assembly of people talking and worshipping God. If someone is apart from them doing that, then I don't think they get the true aspect of church. And that is one of the biggest problems that I have with the actual Catholic Church. I think when Jesus chose the apostles and all that, he had an idea that these were people who were going to be a help. Today, the Pope is supposed to be the biggest helper in the Church. We kind of put him on a pedestal just to listen to everything he says, but I don't think that's what Jesus truly wanted.

Interviewer: *So you think it might have damaged the Church to put the priests on a pedestal.*

> Yeah, very much so. And some of them cannot relate to you when they preach. I've been to so many Masses where the priest during the homily will stand behind the podium, look down, read what he wrote the night before, and get up without any interaction. The priests that have really made a difference in my life are those who actually come off the pulpit, come down and walk around the congregation and make jokes and talk to people during their homily. Almost like telling them a story and involving them in the story. I think that, yeah, a lot of people go to Mass and kind of turn off any type of feeling about religion whatsoever and are just doing what is automatic to them.

From the survey, a twenty-three-year-old woman:

Interviewer: *What do you think are the main qualities that future parish priests should have?*

> I think that a priest needs an open mind, because I think one of the things that is difficult for the Catholic Church is recognizing that most Catholics don't necessarily follow every rule. And, having an understanding approach to that is important. Being accessible to people is important, not just being someone who is based on "This is doctrine." Not just, you now, the rule guy. Rigidity is a bad thing. (laugh) It's a bad thing because you close yourself off to so many opportunities to minister to people

if they don't feel like they can talk to you and come to you and have you listen to them and not judge them. And priests should have humbleness and joy. I know when they get up there into the hierarchy, the archbishops and so on that I've met, they tend to have a lot of pride. And I think that is something that a priest should not have—pridefulness. They do need joy and pride in what they do. That's good, and the desire to be accessible to people.

Interviewer: *Can a lay minister be as strong a leader as a priest?*

No, I don't think so, and I don't think that it would be a good thing necessarily, because for it to be a functional parish, everyone has to have respect for the priest. There should be an open dialogue there. I think, like, deferring to the priest's point of view is good, but collaboration is important. The priest should hear the people. But I think that for respect to be there is important.

A twenty-year-old male student:

Interviewer: *What would be your highest priorities for future priests?*

I guess one important thing for a priest is to be accessible to lay people; to people who aren't very devout but who are exploring their faith. A priest ought to be kind, good with people, friendly, somewhat outgoing, someone who can reach out to others. I think those are pretty important qualities for a priest. I feel like a good priest is also somebody who's a good speaker; somebody who can explain the church. Just a man who's an upstanding person and who is likeable.

Interviewer: *Some priests stress being set apart from laity and others stress collaborating with laity. Do you have any feelings about that?*

I'm definitely in the collaborative camp. I think that the priests should try to be as close to the laity as possible. I remember in our parish we had a priest once who wore as ornate garb as possible during Mass, with as much pomp as he could. And it really put a lot of people off. Not a lot of people really appreciated that. I think the Catholic laity want priests that they can talk to and identify with.

A female college student, twenty-one years old, talks about the qualities of priests she would like to see:

Friendly, funny. Somebody that knows what it's like to be an actual person and not have the priest thing get to their head. Of course, part of this has to be okay with the people too, because a lot of people put priests up on a pedestal. It's hard for them to be an actual person because people say, "He's a priest," when really he's just a person like anybody else. So I think, stressing you are just a person but you're being a representative of God. You can be both, you just have to know the appropriate time for it.

You should not lose your own personality in what you're doing because other people try to see you that *way. I would have whoever is teaching priests stress that you are an actual person and when you are out in public, maybe not wear the collar or something like that, wear regular clothes. Be seen doing stuff with people, not just as the church head. I think people enjoy that, and then they realize that he is just a guy but he's also a priest. Then maybe they will be more attentive.*

Interviewer: *Do you believe that priests should collaborate with the lay people in their ministry?*

Yes, I believe it should be more of a collaborative effort instead of just going in and listening to what the priest has to say and not saying, "Maybe you shouldn't be doing this" or "What you're doing is great; maybe we should do more of this." Listen to the ideas all the way around, everybody listening to everybody else. Sometimes collaborative efforts are the best, but the priest would have to know when they could take charge and make the final decision and when to be collaborative. So many things are collaborative. You can't just decide, "I don't feel we need the carpet, so you're not going to get one," or "I feel we should have a thing for the kids" but the other people don't. Get a vote going.

A twenty-eight-year-old male college student had a different emphasis regarding future priests:

They should be dedicated. Trustworthy. And passionate about it. Those are some of the bigger requirements. You've got to be dedicated to it every day, it doesn't matter how you're feeling or what's going on in your outside world. And you've got to be truthful about it. And that passion; you have to be passionate about God. You can read it in someone's eyes. Priests have that aura around them as if they're just floating—and in their body language. Especially a priest, they're in front of a couple hundred people every day, they need to express that. And then they lead and people follow them.

Interviewer: *Do you think priests should collaborate with laity in their work, or should they be set apart and clearly distinct?*

Clearly distinct. And they should wear uniforms. It's precedent. That's just the way it is.

5

Experiences of Young Lay Ministers

I currently work in the Catholic Church as a Coordinator of Religious Education. I left teaching in the public school system because I felt God was calling me to more directly use my gifts for the good of the Church. It is very exciting to join families on their spiritual journeys and to share with them pivotal moments in their lives as they participate in the Sacraments. I have been given so much, it is only fitting that I give it back to God.

A woman in her 20s

My husband could not be in a youth ministry position in this diocese because the pay is just not there. As far as having a family, no, he could not. He actually used to do youth ministry but got out of it, because he could not continue financially.

A woman in her 20s

Lay ministers don't know if they have a job over the long haul. And there's the whole question of power. The lay ministers' power comes from our degrees and our own lives as disciples; it's not assumed, as with a collar.

A man in his 20s

A few thousand young adults are already working full-time in Catholic lay ministry. How are they faring, and what advice might they offer to the next generation? We have information from three sources. First, we interviewed fifteen full-time lay ministers working in parishes or dioceses throughout the nation, persons recommended to us by our friends and contacts. All were thirty-five or younger, and the majority were working in parishes as youth ministers or young adult ministers. Second, we happened to get twenty-five employed lay ministers in our 2007 diocesan survey. Third, we had a meeting with a group of persons engaged in training lay ministers. These sources of information are not a carefully drawn random sample, so we cannot claim exactness regarding how many people hold which opinions. That is, we are certain that the attitudes we discuss below are real, but we cannot pinpoint how wide ranging they are.

Morale

A main topic is morale. We have been repeatedly asked: how happy are these lay ministers in their jobs? Is morale high or low? Under the circumstances we do not know, mostly because happiness and morale are not easy to assess. The most we can do is to convey the reasons some young lay ministers are happy and others are unhappy.

Beyond doubt, lay ministers are motivated by devotion to God and the Church. They are in the profession out of strong religious commitment and a feeling of being called. They want to make a difference, and they believe that lay ministry is one of the most meaningful things they can do with their lives. Therefore, they are willing to tolerate a certain level of hardship and enforced thrift in order to be privileged to have such jobs. We will look at lay ministers' opinions under seven headings. First, what conditions make for good morale? Second, what conditions make for poor morale? Five other topics are listed later.

(1) Sources of Good Morale

A thirty-three-year-old man:

> *Lay ministers get into this and stay in it because they feel they're responding to a call. It's a vocation with a small v. It's a call from God. It's something where their gifts and talents are well matched. That's the first thing. They do feel that sense of calling that it's not just a job. Secondly, they have the desire to evangelize, to communicate and spread the faith with young people.*

A twenty-nine-year-old woman:

> *One of the joys of us lay ministers, which is kind of exciting, is the breadth of the options. We are almost in the second generation of lay ministers. A lot of the people in ministry are closer to my parents' age, and they were the first generation. They worked to make it be seen as a profession. Now the priests and nuns are not really questioning if we should be in this role, but are giving us a lot more room to develop what that role looks like. Father knows he can't do it all. Lay youth ministers and DREs are kind of an accepted thing. And it's interesting, when I'm talking to my lay ministry friends, the new things that we're able to do. The first generation kind of paved the way and now we're given many opportunities and get involved in things which were always "Father's job."*

A twenty-two-year-old woman:

> These folks are particularly happy, because it's a great opportunity to be working with the church and still be a professional, and fulfill one's vocation in that way. And the key is that folks like myself, we see it not as a job but as a vocation. So we see it as a way to fulfill the mission we've been given by God, that we've been handed. Generally speaking, the folks are delighted to be able to work at something they're so passionate about, such as their faith, their values, and the love for the Church.

Here are comments written by lay ministers from the online survey:

> I am already a lay minister (a DRE). I am in this job because I feel called to it, it is personally very fulfilling, and God has gifted me in many of the skills it requires.

> For me it is a calling. It started as being a volunteer, and through that and the strengthening of my own faith I saw the possibilities. It seemed the natural thing to do. I'd be doing it (Coordinator of Religious Education.) even if I wasn't paid. I'm glad I listened to the Lord. My life is so much more full now.

> My interest is because it is the way I transmit my Catholic faith, through lay ministry with youth and some adults. Actually I am full-time with a minimal salary, but I believe the blessings of God are greater and I feel content to be able to offer guidance to those who need it.

(2) Sources of Poor Morale

We asked what lay ministers complain about when they get together. We heard that the two most common topics are low compensation and the problem of balancing work time with personal time. In the words of a twenty-nine-year-old woman:

> One of the things we find hardest is to find time to balance things in our lives. That's a struggle. I'm single, so I haven't the demands of a family or a spouse, but that probably leads to working too much.
>
> But the other complaint is compensation. It's hard to be paid what perhaps you should be for a master's degree. And job security. Simply being in ministry, there's no guarantee that when you get a new pastor, you're going to still have your job. That's a concern. For those who aren't in parishes, I think it's a little easier.

A twenty-two-year-old woman:

> Usually it's that the work is arduous, there's lots of work, and often the salaries are not commensurate with the working world outside of youth ministry. That tends to come up quite often.

A twenty-three-year-old woman:

> We typically discuss benefits, like insurance. For me myself, I just had a baby, and the insurance benefits were really, really awful as well as the maternity leave. But my pastor was very, very good to me and allowed some maternity leave other than what the diocesan policy was, so he was

very willing to make those arrangements with me. But this doesn't make you think that the parish or diocese really supports family life and growth of the family.

A thirty-one-year-old man talked about problems of boundaries:

Among a lot of the pastors there is not an understanding for what lay ministry is, that the person has a family and must keep healthy boundaries, not so many hours. "No, I have a family. I can't be here 6 a.m. to midnight every day."

A twenty-nine-year-old woman:

The first challenge that comes to my mind is balance between ministry and outside life—coming into lay ministry in an environment which was traditionally dominated by clergy and religious, who pretty much dedicated their lives 24/7 to church. But we're lay people, and I'm a single person, and my vocation is not religious life, not that type of commitment to a community. I need to have that balance of my family, of friends, hopefully a spouse and children—and those kinds of things. Because so much of what we do is answering a call of who we are.

A related topic was brought up in several interviews—relationships with pastors.

A thirty-three-year-old man in a diocesan office:

Another challenge is dealing with pastors. To me, the better pastors know what their limits are. You know, not everybody's an expert in every area of ministry. But plenty of other pastors, instead of setting out a vision and letting people who are expert run with it, they mess with everything, they meddle, they have agendas, and I think that can be very frustrating.

A twenty-six-year-old man spoke about the widespread perceptions of laity:

I think clericalism is the biggest challenge for us. It is ingrained in the Catholic psyche, I think. As soon as most people see a collar, there is an immediate deference, an immediate assumption of authority in matters spiritual. There are also a lot of assumptions that are lined up when a lay person gets up to lead people in prayer, or to lead people into spiritual reflections, or into a space where they talk about their faith. That's probably the biggest challenge.

It's not only in terms of how the congregation perceives lay ministers, but how the hierarchy perceives us. I know that the bishops, in their latest statement on lay ministry, had a large discussion as to whether to call us "ministers" at all. I know that three bishops argued against that; they are all conservative bishops. They argued that if we used the word "minister," people will confuse us with priests. I think this argument is widespread among the bishops. I don't think it is an issue on the pastoral level, on the level of people and ministers at a parish. But clericalism does come up: practically, who is in charge? And in the fact that tomorrow the next pastor could come and fire the entire staff or totally change policies that we've built and worked so hard for. And that's probably the most frustrating part of this whole job.

A thirty-three-year-old man:

Another thing would be a lack of respect for lay ministry. You know, this is a profession and a vocation, but sometimes it's viewed as "You work for the church. When are you going to get a real job?"

Here are typical comments written on the online survey:

I am currently a professional in the Catholic Church and I am finding that there is too much expected of me, with no rewards in career advancement or pay for my ambition and hard work. In short, working as a lay minister in the Catholic Church, one faces a concrete ceiling.

I currently am a full-time lay minister (youth minister). I love it because I'm living out my faith, helping teens, and getting to be creative. The pay is horrible though. I'm not sure how long I can afford to do it.

I am currently involved in full-time ministry work because: 1) I feel called to it. 2) I can share the love God has shown me through others. 3) I can use my talents to serve the church. I fear that it will not be long-term, that I will not be able to provide for my young family with the small income available and that the income-to-education ratio is lopsided compared to the private sector. I worry that I will not be effective in the long run because I will not be able to continue. I believe this hurts the Church.

Four Other Topics

(3) Is Lay Ministry Temporary or Permanent?

We have heard some Catholic voices say that lay ministry is temporary until we get more priests. When that happens, we will no longer need lay ministers. Did the interviewees agree? No. Had they heard this argument? Yes, most had. A thirty-three-year-old man:

> I hear it occasionally from lay Catholics who are very clerical-centered, and I think they're a small percentage. But I don't think anybody sees the number of active clergy rising again to look like it did in the 1940s or something, any time soon. I think it's a very small minority who actually believe that, and even a small minority of priests who believe that. They know that the demographics have changed and the role of the priest has changed as a result, especially in terms of the administrative functions that so many of them did.

A twenty-six-year-old man:

> I have heard the argument, but only from the very conservative faction. I've not heard it from anybody in my parish. It's the view of only the minority. The fact is, the shortage of priests has the upside that the layperson is finally taking on his or her role in the church, actually working and ministering to the needs of the community.

A twenty-seven-year-old woman:

> Yes, I've heard that. I couldn't begin to fathom who thinks like that. The Second Vatican Council made it very clear that lay ecclesial ministry was not only something they supported, but it is something that was needed. And so unless someone's been living under a rock and hasn't read any of the church documents, they would know that it's something that's supported from the larger scale, not as a need to fill places because of a shortage of priests, but they would realize that the church is made of many different types of people and when you have different types of people working in the church you can relate better.
>
> The culture here in [the Midwest] is that we have lay ministry. This is just part of where we are. The priests at least in our archdiocese recognize that they can't do it all. They rely very heavily on their lay ministers to work collaboratively with them to minister to the parish.

A twenty-nine-year-old woman:

> Yeah, I have heard it. It makes me laugh. I think it's a nostalgic desire not to have to acknowledge a priest shortage and say that then we wouldn't need this. But even if we had a huge resurgence in priests, I think there are still lay men and women who are committed to being an active part of the ministry. And I find that shocking. It's somewhat dismissive. It is one of the challenges of doing ministry. "You're just a stopgap for the church." If you're a youth minister it is, "You're just a person that plays with kids," or

"You're just figuring out whether you want to be a nun or not," as if the only way it is permitted that you be in this ministry, if you are en route to somewhere else.

(4) Does the Development of Lay Ministry Threaten Priests?

Our interviews included this topic because we repeatedly heard it discussed. It is sometimes alleged that development of lay ministries threatens the clergy-lay distinction and that promotion of lay ministry with young men reduces the number going to the seminary. The prevailing response among the young lay ministers we talked with was that they had heard discussions of priests feeling threatened, but they thought the problem could be addressed. A twenty-nine-year-old woman:

I haven't had anyone tell me that, but I have friends who have heard that. It's a little different version of "You shouldn't be doing that, that's Father's job." But priests don't have a problem with that. Very rarely have I run across a member of the clergy who feels that they're being usurped. Much more it's members of the parish. They say, "Father used to . . ." That's the catchword for all of those things. Older people say that. But for younger people, we're accepted.

Religious women and deacons have been more easily accepted. At least they're "kind of" religious. (laugh) Married women coming in, that's a little bit harder. That's not something the people have experienced. But it seems that parishes really adapt and thrive, and it's because of the competence and knowledge of the lay minister. There are going to be people who do not like the fact that Father is not here. Of course they want a priest. That's a loss for them, and there's a grieving process. But how can we adjust to this? I think there are always going to be places that are anti-layperson in the parish, but depending on the skill of that person, that changes.

A thirty-three-year-old man:

I think the priests who are secure in their priesthood and in the call that they felt called to pursue, they're not threatened by lay ministers. It's just priests who are insecure or immature, young or old, I think they are the ones that get a bit rattled. I think we see a bit of that with the new ultraconservative religious orders, they're the ones who feel threatened by lay ministry. Let's face it, they want a real clerical-focused church leadership. Most of the priests I work with are not like that. For them, they view themselves first and foremost as sacramental ministers and unifiers. Being administrators is way down their list now. They find other people who are better at that, who have the gifts to do those sorts of things.

A twenty-six-year-old man:

I have heard it, but I don't understand why we need to keep that clergy-lay distinction so sharp. But when we promote lay ministry, it needs to work toward collaboration; I would not advocate it if it's working against the priesthood. I'm not against the priesthood unless it becomes a church that elevates the priesthood above everybody else instead of putting it at the service of the church.

A twenty-two-year-old woman:

I have heard the argument on occasion. When I've heard that coming from priests, it's particularly from priests who have come here from other countries. In other countries there still is a huge gap between clergy and lay ministers; in other words, they're not treated on an equal plane. So when I've heard priests say these things, it's from priests from countries where they're still on the pedestal.

A twenty-three-year-old women:

I haven't heard that. In my parish I don't see that, because the laity pretty much runs the parish here for him so that he can do his pastoral duties and whatnot.

A twenty-nine-year-old man:

No, the priests are not threatened. The priests are grateful for the lay ministers they work with. There is certainly an acknowledgement in their hearts that the ministry has changed over the years. The younger priests don't remember the days when each parish had two or three priests.

A thirty-one-year-old man:

I have heard that, and I know that some people do feel that way. With our clergy, if part of their formation would be on the re-emergence of lay ministry and the importance of it, we would have a better chance to have some greater understanding. And also with regard to lay ministry formation, it needs an understanding of what lay ministers are called to do, how it is different from the gifts that the clergy bring, and how we need the two in the church to work together. So, from both sides, we can overcome the problem.

(5) Problems of Turnover and Burnout

We heard many accounts of high turnover rates, especially among youth ministers. Two interviewees said that on the average, youth ministers and young adult ministers change jobs every two or three years. In other lay ministry jobs, the turnover rate is lower, yet still high enough to be a concern.

A thirty-three-year-old man:

The average youth minister does not last more than three years in the field. It's not very long, and therefore it makes it very hard to convince people to pay reasonably and to go get training. A lot of it's dominated by twenty-something-year-olds just out of college, and they've got that missionary zeal kind of thing. They do it for a few years and then they discover that they can't make any money, so they leave!

That's not everybody, but that's a common thing. You get youthful energy, but you don't get staying power. And other people who might be a little bit older don't last because of the frustrations. They think going to work for the church is going to be like being in a gospel story of sitting with the apostles, and they discover that there's

> *power struggles, there's politics, people are mean and nasty, and they fight about money, and so they get very disillusioned and leave.*

A twenty-seven-year-old woman:

> *I think the turnover is a big problem in lay ministry. It's even higher in youth ministry, but it's true across the board. I think there's a high rate, mostly going from one church to another, kind of bouncing around, because there's no sense of stability in some places.*

Interviewer: *Is there a general sense that youth ministry and young adult ministry is a young people's profession?*

> *Oh yeah, I hear that all the time! "Oh, you're so lucky you're so young. You can relate to the teens." But I don't feel that's true. Some of the best youth ministers I know are in their fifties, and they're incredible at what they do. So I don't think it's an age thing. It is passion and a vocation. I don't think because you're young you automatically relate better to youth.*

A twenty-three-year-old woman:

> *There's a lot of turnover, yeah. It could become a problem, because teenagers need consistency, and without that you typically don't have the rapport that you need to really influence their lives. Typically it takes some time. When people come in and out, you really don't get the job done—depending on what you're doing.*

Several persons linked turnover with personal burnout. They observed that young lay ministers often come with high enthusiasm and then become frustrated when the leadership does not support their ideas. Other young persons work night and day and in a year or two are exhausted. A twenty-six-year-old man:

> I think burnout is a problem in parish life in general. Ministers need to be aware that they need to take care of themselves; that it's very easy to come in to the office in the early morning and stay till the evening, because lots of things happen at night at parishes. So it's easy not to take time for themselves, especially if you're a giving person. I've found that I take time during the day for prayer, and make sure that when I go home I relax with the TV (laugh). And get good sleep and eat well. And no matter what, take my days off.

A twenty-nine-year-old man:

> All of us are in ministry because we want to make a difference, and we want to dedicate ourselves to the work of Christ and the church. There's always more work to be done, and it's always important to make decisions about what work can get done with your time and with your energy. There are colleagues of mine in my field who do not have a regular day off! They overdo it because it's important work, and they see the need for it and they feel called to it. But there needs to be a balance between viewing the work both as ministry and also as job. And part of professional work is taking vacations

*and making sure you have a couple of days off a week.
Part of the problem is tradition. Our church was built on
the shoulders of priests and nuns who didn't always have
a day off.*

A thirty-year-old man complained about some pastors:

*You come into the church with a good heart and trying
to do good work, but the politics of the church is what
gets you . . . the power-tripping of the priests. You think
it's about Jesus, but they make it about them. People
who are in positions just for the sake of having positions.
Young people come in there trying to help, but they get
turned off because they see almost hypocrisy.*

(6) The Predominance of Females

In our interviews we referred to the recent survey of lay ecclesial ministers conducted by David DeLambo that found that
eighty percent are female (DeLambo, 45). We asked everyone
whether this eighty percent is proper or whether it is a problem. We heard arguments in both directions. Some thought it
was good. A twenty-six-year-old man:

*The eighty percent is just symptomatic of our culture, that
religion is women's business. I think it's great, actually,
especially since women in the Catholic Church have not
had roles like this in the past, not even nuns. They've been
teachers or been cloistered. But now all these opportunities are opening up for different types of lay ministers,
not just DREs or principals, but associate pastors [sic] or*

pastoral administrators. Really, women who are pastors. I think it's wonderful.

A twenty-nine-year-old man:

I think it's good that there are large numbers of women in lay ministry. It counterbalances the very male hierarchy of the church. It is, in part, because the field of ministry is underpaid, and men cannot support a family in lay ministry. Similar to teaching and nursing, where there were more women than men, with low compensation.

An argument on the other side, that more men are needed, was voiced repeatedly. A thirty-three-year-old man:

In the parish it's very difficult to motivate teenage boys to participate in something that the equivalent of their mom is running. Some of it is the role model mentorship thing. Some of it is just the basic thing of setting an example. We [in the diocese] have many female youth ministers and many male youth ministers, and many of them both do a good job. I have noticed that with the male youth ministers, they tend to have a better proportion—more boys present. Girls still outnumber them, but more boys come.

I think youth groups need to have a mix of boys and girls. In my own church I run the youth group, and I try to have at least 40 percent guys, because some guys who would want to be involved, aren't, for social reasons, at least among the teenagers I work with. But getting men youth ministers is not easy.

A twenty-three-year-old women:

> *It is a problem. I think it's because unfortunately the money just isn't there for the head of a household to be in a lay ministry position. Not around here. Until the money situation improves, there won't be many more males. It would be better if half were men, because we all bring different qualities. And there are some roles that men are better at than women, and vice versa.*

Recommendations to Strengthen Lay Ministry

In all our interviews we asked the person to imagine that he or she had been picked to speak to the bishops and other Church leaders about how to strengthen lay ministry. What would he or she say? The interviewees were sometimes taken aback by the question, and not everyone had a ready answer. Yet after some quick thinking and stop-and-start expressions, everybody made recommendations.

We heard four themes, listed here more or less in descending order of emphasis. (A) Most common, they asked for better appreciation and support for lay ministry. (B) They requested more opportunities for spiritual development. (C) They asked for more financial support. (D) They asked for more credentialing. Here are some examples:

(A) Better appreciation and support for lay ministry

A twenty-nine-year-old woman:

> *Most lay ministers come in expecting to be considered professionals and a valuable part of the staff, that people*

on the staff will feel that I have something to give. But then I felt like I always wasn't enough because I wasn't a priest or a nun. We need a certain acknowledging of the gifts and talents that the lay minister can bring to the staff. The people who are happiest in their lay ministry are the ones who have good working relationships with their supervisors and have the ability to get good positive, constructive feedback.

Particularly as a young person, there are stereotypes and challenges that you face just coming out of college. There are stereotypes anywhere, but particularly in church. You're always "that kid." But if the pastor gives support and says, "Well, I hired her; she gave you her answer. I have confidence in her," and "Why are you circumventing her to come to me? She's my staff," that is what we want. We want supervision. And clergy aren't always that good at it. They weren't trained for it. I think my pastor has no idea of what to do with us in terms of supervision. Something he was never taught to do when he was ordained forty years ago.

A twenty-two-year-old woman:

I think we have to market the opportunity to serve professionally in the Catholic Church and also ask for more support from the bishops and folks in the top echelon. Not many people know about "Co-Workers in the Vineyard," and they need to know that we need their talent and willingness to serve, and their passion. And so, get the word out that the church as a whole, especially the clergy, is fully in support of lay ministers. People don't know that. And people don't know that we are considered as valuable by our bishops.

A twenty-six-year-old man had specific as well as general recommendations:

There are vocations committees in every parish. I wonder how many of those vocations committees are promoting lay ministry. Not many. I have heard only one parish, at the prayers of the faithful, praying for vocations for lay ministry—one parish out of the many parishes that I know, in [this diocese]. People just don't think of it. Normally, on the parish level, people don't think to promote vocations to the lay ministry.

We need to be more respected, and we need to be introduced to the parish. I really have not been introduced publicly to the parish here. It should be a normal thing, but it wasn't done here. There even should be some sort of rite of commission for us.

A thirty-six-year-old man:

Here in [this diocese] I'm looking for us to look at how we recruit, train, develop, form, and educate lay ecclesial ministers in as centralized and comprehensive a process as it is for seminarians to become priests and even for the permanent diaconate program. I think we might need to look at the merits of looking at lay ecclesial ministers in the same way.

I would have liked some sort of ceremony when I started work here. I think that's appropriate. Not anything big and extravagant. Unfortunately, in my parish, we don't even do that for the parish council, which in every other place I've ever worked or been assigned to, that was the norm. And make them visible. I'm a big fan of the pictures on the wall of both the staff and the parish council. I'm a big fan of a blessing or welcoming or investing ritual. And then when people leave, for whatever reason, a sending forth ... just like we do with priests and pastors.

(B) More opportunities for spiritual development

A woman, age twenty-seven:

I think we need to provide more ongoing spiritual development for our lay ministers. I feel we sometimes do so much planning retreats and planning prayer experiences for those that we work with, we don't take enough time for ourselves, so I think we should be able to provide retreat opportunities or spiritual direction opportunities, theological reflection opportunities for lay ministers.

A man, age twenty-six:

Teach us how to pray. Give us adequate formation, a good education, both beforehand and on the job. Have formation and education for people on the job. And support groups. Have groups of them gather, maybe small faith-sharing groups but also professional development, all of that. And that is being done to some extent now.

A twenty-five-year-old woman:

There needs to be an increase in formation models, where laypeople and those preparing for ordination study side by side from the get-go. Because I think in twenty-five years you're going to have lay people who are trained with lay people and ordained who are trained just with the ordained, with separate warring ecclesiologies, perhaps, and both struggling with the language to work with the other. And I think sometimes we laypeople place all of the blame for that on our priests, and I think, wait a minute, we're equally as guilty if we make snap judgments about them. I think that's something the U.S. bishops need to start addressing.

(C) More financial support

A twenty-nine-year-old woman:

Salaries are a serious question. I think there is a justice issue. We understand that we work for the church, and so we understand that this is not a field which you're going into to make money. You're never going to be rich in this ministry, but as a church that advocates for a working wage and for a just salary, and that people should not be struggling to pay their bills, we should probably, as a church, evidence that in the people we employ. We're not just volunteers doing this as a second job.

Clergy make sacrifices in order to do ministry, and in the same way there are sacrifices that lay people make in order to do this ministry. And our church deserves people who are well-educated, well-formed, competent ministers. And that's what you're asking me to be, and if I need to be that person in order to be qualified to minister, then I would think you have the same responsibility to help me attain that, as you would with your clergy, and pay me enough.

The recommendations regarding finances were not only requests for higher salaries in order to reduce turnover, but also for a higher priority on youth ministry and young adult ministry in parish life. This was mentioned by two persons. An example, from a man aged thirty-three:

We definitely are still behind the curve of the Protestant evangelical churches, for sure. For them, a youth minister is a second or third priority. A lot of them have full-time youth ministers. For them it's the pastor, then the person in charge of the music, then the youth person. Those are their top three hires. I read about that routinely in youth ministry publications. For them it's a priority, consistently across the board. They throw money and resources at it. And for us—not all Catholic parishes, but for a lot—it's still a luxury item. It's still an "extra," it's not viewed as a necessity when dividing up the financial pie.

(D) More credentialing

A thirty-three-year-old man:

> *Push to make lay ministry more professional. Get standard professional qualifications and evaluations. If bishops promoted that to themselves and to their pastors, it would help professionalize and standardize lay ministry. Right now it's kind of like whatever the latest fad is, is called "ministry."*

A twenty-seven-year-old woman:

> *I think we are moving along, but it's going to take a little bit of time. I think the certification processes that are coming out of the [National Association] for Lay Ecclesial Ministers are an excellent step.*

A twenty-nine-year-old woman:

> *I think for the future, credentials for lay ministry really should be a necessity. I think we've moved beyond that time in which people just fell into a field. There's a certain expectation of competence and of knowledge and professional academic understanding. But sometimes we get so busy just trying to fill a spot, we have an opening and we want to fill it with a person. We really need to look at the fact that this is a different kind of job. There needs to be a spiritual match and a theological match.*

Reports from Institutions Training Lay Ministers

We were able to hold a focus group with six administrators of lay training programs in different regions of the nation. We discussed numerous issues. The educators were all in agreement on three topics, and this seems noteworthy.

First, in general there is an adequate supply of candidates for the available lay ministry jobs. The supply varies by job category, but the only category that may not have enough good candidates is youth ministry. Otherwise there are enough lay people who want the jobs out there.

Second, the profession of lay ministry needs more young people. The average age is too high now. Young people would bring new vigor and would be a sign that lay ministry has a future. They would also be key for better ministry to youth and young adults. The most valuable young people would be persons who see ministry as a calling and a long-term career.

Third, everyone reported a new trend toward a more conservative ecclesiology among students. Recent lay ministry students, that is, are trending toward traditionalism, much like the often-discussed trend among seminarians. For example, a man from the West Coast:

> We are seeing more and more laypeople in the past three or four years who are more "clerical" or "hierarchical." I've seen them become much more conservative. In the intake interviews, I ask them, "Who are you reading?" and they're into reading Scott Hahn. They don't talk about Lonergan or Rahner and say they want to

study them more. Many of them are coming from the apologetic standpoint and want to learn the answers.

In the final chapter of this book we return to the attitudes of college students and active young adults—no longer looking only at persons working as lay ministers. We asked our online survey respondents what they recommended for the future direction of the Church, and they jumped at the opportunity to be heard, as we will see in Chapter 6.

6

Recommendations: The Future of the Catholic Church

I believe the Catholic Church really needs to focus on the young adults in the church. We lose so many young people to other religions because of lack of energy in music, sermons, social activity, everything!! If we were to focus on our young adults, the faith of the Catholic Church would be more deeply planted in young people, therefore causing a more devout relationship to God as well as with people.

A woman in her 20s

I feel that the Church needs to go back to its roots. It needs to live the way the magisterium teaches. The church needs to separate itself from contemporary teachings and become the solid foundation it once was. I believe the main problem in the Catholic Church is that people do not want to offend anyone. After all, Christ himself said that He did not come to bring peace but rather to turn sons against fathers and daughters against mothers.

A man in his 20s

The Catholic Church in the years ahead should change with the times. It seems right now that we are going backwards with the changes the bishops and pope have recently implemented. We need to change with the times—we can still keep our rituals, but things must change.

A man in his 30

What would young adult Catholics like to see in the Church's future? What would they recommend to the Vatican and the bishops? We asked them directly in our surveys:

"Catholic leaders are interested in hearing the views of many people. In your opinion, what should be the direction of the Catholic Church in the years ahead? What should the Church stress, and how should it move? What would you recommend?"

The respondents were asked to write in their ideas. Their answers show that they welcomed this invitation. They had plenty of time to ponder, since with an online survey there is no rush and no time limit. Most persons wrote two to ten lines of text with one or two main ideas. Women wrote more than men. We read all the responses, both English and Spanish, and grouped them in fourteen categories. When respondents made several recommendations, we coded the two that were most emphasized.

Nobody should expect that the people in the samples would agree with each other on these topics. Young adults are diverse. Some respondents were directly opposed to others,

Table 6.1

Recommended Direction of the Catholic Church in the Years Ahead (up to two codes in any response; in percents)

	College Sample	Diocesan Sample
Number of responses:	(340)	(373)
More focus on youth, college students, and young adults	23	21
Go back to tradition; reject modern teaching; don't water down the faith	12	17
Relate more to modern life; relate to changing times, e.g., in music and morals	11	9
More lay ministry; more empowerment of lay people	9	17
Accept married priests	9	10
Stress love and forgiveness, not strict rules; accept all people, e.g., homosexuals	8	10
Accept women priests	6	6
Better religious education and catechesis	5	10
No change in rules; reject married priests and women priests	5	5
Teach traditional morals; reject contraception, homosexuality, premarital sex	4	5
More stress on sacraments, Eucharist, or Mass	3	6
More evangelization and outreach	3	5
More emphasis on the poor and oppressed; more social justice	3	4
More ecumenism; more tolerance of other faiths	3	2

for example on the question of married priests or the question of rethinking moral teachings on sex and gender. Table 6.1 shows our fourteen categories in descending order of frequency for the college sample.

In both samples, the main recommendation was that the Church should put more focus on youth, college students, and young adults. This idea ranked far ahead of others.

The second and third most frequent recommendations were on both sides of the question of understanding tradition. The second stressed "go back to tradition; reject modern teaching; don't water down the faith," while the third stressed the opposite: "relate more to modern life; relate to changing times, for example, in music and morals." This tells us that young Catholics are divided in their views about holding to tradition versus adapting to modern life. A few more stressed holding to tradition than stressed flexibility in conveying the faith.

The fourth most common recommendation was to expand lay ministry and give more empowerment to lay people; it was emphasized more among the diocesan sample than among the college students.

The fifth, seventh, and eighth were about priests. The fifth said to accept married priests and the seventh said to accept women priests, while the eighth said the opposite—to have no change in rules and in particular no acceptance of married priests and women priests. The young adults are divided in their attitudes, with more in favor of married priests and women priests than against them.

The sixth stressed love and forgiveness on moral issues rather than adherence to strict rules, and to be more accepting of all people, for example, homosexuals.

Other recommendations were less commonly voiced, including better religious education and catechesis, stress on traditional morals on sexual matters, more evangelization, more concern for the poor, and more ecumenism. In this chapter we will scrutinize the most-voiced recommendations.

Five Main Areas of Recommendations

Put simply, the top five recommendations were (1) more attention to youth, college students, and young adults; (2a and 2b—two sides of a single issue) go back to tradition versus relate more to changing times; (3) more lay ministry and empowerment of lay people; (4a and 4b—again two sides) accepting or rejecting married priests and women priests; and (5) stressing love, forgiveness, and acceptance rather than strict rules. Of the five most-mentioned themes, three convey a near-unanimity of opinion, while two themes are divided into conflicting opinions. We will look at each of the five.

(1) More attention to youth, college students, and young adults

This topic was mentioned more often than any other. The high frequency of mentions was not cued by anything in our online survey; it represents a genuine research finding. As we will see, opinions were basically in agreement. First, here are some writings by college students. Some were written in Spanish, but they are reported here in English translation.

> If there is anything I would like to see, it would be to see more ministries available to young adults ages 20–30. It almost seems as if sometimes we are excluded. Other ministries are either too young or too old. If we could balance this out, I think many things would change for the good.

> Helping young individuals at the college and high school level grow closer to God is essential in the expansion of

the Catholic Church. During this period I believe many people grow farther away from God because of all of the temptations, and there are no parental figures to look over you really. Being engaged in activities with followers of God takes the temptations away from the adolescents and young adults.

I think that the Church really needs to stress more for teens and young adults. Many large parish churches, especially my own, do not have much for people after confirmation. My mother and I have been working hard to try and establish something in my church, but it is difficult. I love my Newman Center. I wish we could have something like this within my own home parish.

I would like to see the Church worldwide empower youth and young adults to internalize the words of Pope John Paul II that young people are not "the future of the Church," but rather they ARE the Church. I would like to see church leaders stress the importance of youth and young adult ministry and the inclusion of young adults in the life and ministry of the Church.

The Church needs to be more conscious of its youth, who are leaving the Church in droves because of its failure to appeal to their sensibilities, intelligence, and morality.

The church should stress youth ministry. The media is trying to tear us from our faith, and teens and young adults are most impressionable and likely to lose their faith because of peer pressure or the urge to fit in. I personally lost my faith when the youth ministry failed at my church, and have yet to find a ministry where I feel as comfortable sharing my faith and feelings. Youth ministry needs to be a second home and family, not a class or requirement.

From the diocesan sample:

The Church needs to reach out to the youth and to rekindle the passion for Christ that should burn so fervently, but is often snuffed out by rules and regulations.

The Church really needs to focus on getting youth and young adults involved! Getting involved has changed my life! I originally strayed from the Church because I did not feel connected to it. Why are Protestant churches so much better at offering fellowship and Bible studies, etc., than we are? This time is crucial! Young adults often make decisions that affect the rest of their lives at this point! They need to be targeted. The Church really needs to make young adults understand that they are needed, they can make a difference, and that the Church cares about them.

I wholeheartedly believe that the future of the Church rests in our ability to foster a passion for Christ within the youth. This is not to suggest that the rest of the laity should be of less importance, but to address the vocation crisis and the issue of young adults leaving the Church.

The church should stress getting our young people involved in all aspects of the church. We have basically left them out there in society with nothing to hold on to. We do not teach how to defend our faith to those who say, "Have you been saved by Jesus Christ?" I got to college and was so overwhelmed with the other faiths and the fundamental churches trying to get me to change. It was so easy to join them because they were fun and hip, but eventually I came back to my own roots in the Catholic faith.

(2a) Relate more to modern life and changing times

These comments talked about modernizing moral teachings, music, and worship, but they did not advocate any change in the core teachings of Catholicism. Here are typical statements, first from the college student sample:

The way I see it, the trouble with the Catholic Church is that it tries to simultaneously embrace the values of openness and freedom of expression while still holding steadfast to certain viewpoints and philosophies, some of which are egregiously out of date. The Catholic leadership needs to sit down and draw up an unambiguous stance on the most essential issues facing the Church, leaving only personal matters up to free interpretability, unless it is content to continue to sacrifice its credibility in the name of vagueness.

I absolutely love the Mass I attend. They have a band and go against the "traditional" mass that I attended as a child. My recommendation is to keep the church changing with the times.

I consider myself conservative, but I think the Church is holding on to rules that do not apply to today's world any more. They should start moving forward and change the outdated laws.

I know that the Catholic Church is rooted in tradition, but it needs to change a little to go with the times. I wish I could see more priests on fire with their calling instead of tired old men who've forgotten what they stand for. I wish women could have a chance to be priests. I wish priests would stop abusing children. I wish we could get rid of that Catholic guilt and fill people with the joy and abundance that is Jesus Christ.

The changes that I believe the Catholic Church should make are too numerous to list here, but I will emphasize the most important things. The Catholic Church should probably loosen its ties to tradition a little bit, since we live in a changing world where the views of the Catholic Church tend to alienate certain people.

From the diocesan sample:

The Catholic Church should lead us through dynamic liturgy, programs, events, and outreach. The Mass should relate to the people by having every parish offer everything from contemporary to upbeat music and messages that are directed to the young and old. The

Church should stress involvement by engaging more of its people through dynamic music and liturgy that meets the people from where they are at and leads them closer to Jesus in their hearts and minds through the Eucharist. Let's be honest and upfront with the people. We all have made and make mistakes. Let's talk about how we can improve our lives and live them to the fullest without making anyone feel they are not welcomed because they have sinned.

I believe the world is changing, and if the church doesn't make some change, it will become lost.

I feel that many of the ways of the Catholic Church are old and outdated. I think we need to keep with tradition and all of the morals and values while putting a fresher, more updated portrayal of them. So much of the music is slow and uninspiring. It should be a celebration of who we are and what we believe. We need to find more ways to motivate people under forty. So many of the groups and speeches are geared for the older generations. I find that Church leadership tends to feel that the youth of the church just doesn't care about Church—but what is being done to motivate the youth, to keep them interested and attending?

It should cater more to young people and be a little less strict but not too much. It should convey the morals in a more modern manner, which would encourage others to become Catholic.

I want a church more in tune with the times in which we live, tending to actual problems, a church more spiritual and less bureaucratic, a church where Jesus would feel present.

(2b) Go back to tradition
From college students:

Any move of the Church should always be initiated by the Holy Spirit, always in keeping with the original teachings of Jesus Christ and never out of outside pressure from the media, the "demands of the times," special interest groups, modernism, liberalism, relativism, etc. If there is a change that must be made, the Holy Spirit will indicate in which direction to go. Let the Church not be moved by the winds of change of the world—which come and go—but let it be moved by the winds of the Holy Spirit.

Stay traditional. Jesus himself started our church, and we have no right to change it. Get back to Vatican II teaching!

The Catholic Church should maintain its reliance on tradition and truly follow doctrine. If Catholic leaders (priests, religious, and laity) were to teach the real truth, then imagine how the world and the people may be inspired to change.

The Church should maintain its long-standing traditions, positions on social issues, and vocations. There should be a return to a conservative liturgy and reverence within Mass.

From the diocesan sample:

A return to the old Latin rite! The Mass is too liberal and irreverent. Also, the Church needs to take a harder stance on our beliefs. There is too much backing down on important issues, and the world doesn't take us seriously because of it.

Stay true to its teaching, that of the Lord. Don't be swayed by secular or popular beliefs. Be the calm in the storm.

Strongly, boldly and compassionately proclaim the teachings of Christ and his Church. A return to orthodoxy is needed by priests, religious, and seminarians—then the lay people will follow when we see it lived out by those God has chosen to lead. Bishops need to be appointed who are strong moral leaders and are not shy in the proclamation of the truth of the Church.

The Church and priests in general should focus on the doctrinal teachings and stop watering them down. I believe that this, as opposed to leaning toward relaxing disciplines or ignoring difficult teachings, tends to disinterest folks.

A whole generation of Catholics seem to be unaware of the basic truths of our faith, like the Church's teaching on abortion, homosexuality, and marriage and divorce. A good number of Catholics don't even know that the Eucharist is the true Body, Blood, Soul, and Divinity of our Lord Jesus Christ! No wonder they leave the Church as they do. Catholic leaders need to be fearless in teaching the Gospel of our Lord Jesus Christ no matter what the cost, because in the end, more souls will be saved.

(3) More lay ministry and empowerment of lay people

This recommendation was mentioned especially often by the persons in the diocesan sample. First, here is a sample of college student opinions:

I would recommend fostering an environment that makes lay leadership more accessible and less daunting, especially among women.

I think they need to give women more responsibility. The church is in desperate need for people to serve, and this could be a way to help.

There is a great need for charismatic, educated people working in lay ministry. While a priest may be a vibrant leader and teacher in the faith, not all priests have these gifts. Further, while the priest is necessary to provide the sacraments to a faith community, lay people can work together with the clergy to revitalize and enrich it. For the Church this means creating jobs. These jobs must pay sufficient to support a family.

The lay ministry needs to be empowered faster and fuller. The future of the church is largely in lay ministry, and can provide a refreshing new accessibility in the church.

From the diocesan sample:

I love God and my faith, but I strongly disagree with the leadership. Not theological issues, but on the hypocrisies of the leadership. My biggest beef against the church is its inability to change because of its fear of sharing "power." There are many people who are competent, credible, and faithful who can lead and want to participate in creating a better future.

I believe that there is a crisis at hand with the dwindling number of ordained priests. Although I don't particularly like the idea of the Church changing doctrine to accommodate the current social situation of the world, something obviously has to be done to keep the faith vibrant. I believe that parishes should tap into their lay population as much as possible to relieve the overburdened priests as much as possible.

Increasing the involvement and power of laity would be an important step. The Church does not belong to Rome or to men in vestments. This Church belongs to all of us. The more we act like we understand this, the better.

If we do not embrace the gift of the laity as equal ministers, we are losing a major component of the Church. And if we continue to downplay the importance of women and lay people in the Church, we cannot then ask why no one is getting involved.

I think we need to move to a lay-empowered church, stressing inclusivity and togetherness. I'd LOVE to see married persons and women as priests in my lifetime, and in my opinion, this is the only way the Catholic Church is going to survive in our generation.

I would encourage the church to empower the current full-time ministry staff at a parish to include and positively engage the laity in helping to meet the needs of the parish. Currently it seems the direction of the church is held in the hands of the local pastor, and though thoughts are requested, they are often implemented very slowly and often in a way very frustrating for a young person to be involved. The church must open up its arms to welcome more laity to support parishes and move beyond a one-person staff to engage the youth or other areas of ministry.

I am a "sometimes Catholic" but very involved in my church, but only because it has lay "talk-back" times during the homily, lay preaching teams (even with a priest present), and the laity can truly run the show. I think that the seminary culture and education must be rethought, as well as the entire model of clericalism, official and unofficial. It just doesn't resonate with the vast majority of young adults out here, nor does it encourage diversity within active church ranks. Not enough priests and bishops are brave enough to stick their necks out, and the entire church culture is sorely lacking from true, inspired leadership. A lot of policing at the top means the rest of us are starving and looking for food in other areas.

The Catholic Church needs to promote lay ministry and the fact that at baptism all of us are called to ministry. Even if we do not choose ministry as a vocation, we are called to minister to one another throughout our lives in many ways—day to day. The Catholic Church needs to be more open to the gifts that all people have to offer, not just me. Encourage married men to be involved and to be husbands and fathers as Christ is the groom of the Church. Equal pay for equal work in lay ministry is also necessary for women and all lay ministers in the church. It is unfortunate that we lose so many passionate ministers because they cannot afford to raise their family (or even send their kids to Catholic schools) on the salary paid by the church.

Prepare laypersons in diverse ecclesiastical jobs, but be VERY cautious in selecting these persons, because their academic training does not necessarily make a person more prepared for an ecclesiastical position.

(4a) Rejecting married priests and women priests

First we present a sample of the written-in comments rejecting the concept of married priests and women priests, then the comments in favor. The persons approving of married priests and women priests far outnumber the number in opposition.

First, here is a sample of the college student comments rejecting married priests and women priests:

> *Definitely stress the importance of leadership positions in the Church, especially building blocks like the priesthood. The Church does not need to give in to internal and external pressure to change fundamental teachings (i.e., a priest may not need to practice celibacy, women in the priesthood, etc.). I personally think it will be especially trying in the years to come for the Church and its people, but the Church must never compromise its teaching.*

> *I think the church needs to get back to its tradition more. I'm not stressing Pius the Tenth or anything, but I think more structure and stronger enforcement of rules would be a good thing. Priests should not get married. They are married to Christ and they made a lifelong commitment to him and to serve his people.*

> *In today's society many people are calling for married priests, female priests, and duration priests (for a certain amount of time). We as a church must remember the theological reasons the priesthood is the way it is and stick to it. We have survived this long and will continue to do so. Changing the core of our beliefs and practices is in some way admitting that we are defeated. WE ARE NOT. The world will try to take us, but they will not prevail.*

The Church needs to regain its Catholic focus. American Catholics are especially losing grasp of what it means to be Catholic. We need an increased respect for the clergy and an increase in vocational awareness. The religious life should be viewed with respect and encouragement. A renewal in the Church needs to begin from the top down. Ordaining married priests or replacing priestly positions with lay ministers are not solutions. These fixes will only lead to a greater loss of our Catholic identity.

From the diocesan sample:

The Catholic Church should stand as a beacon of truth in a very distorted culture. The Church should not cater to people's desires for sex and money. The priest needs to reclaim his position as a spiritual shepherd, not an administrator or events coordinator. The priest should be focused on the Eucharist and other sacraments along with prayer. The laity should support the priest with prayer, organization, and administration. Also, emphasize the obligation of lay people to live contemplative lives, similar to those of religious orders. Promote religious vocations without compromise. Show that religious life allows a unity with God that marriage or a married priesthood cannot provide.

The Church needs to continue to respond to the indications of the Holy Spirit—the Church is a dynamic living thing that is constantly responding to God's gradually unfolding plan and will. The Church should stress faithfulness. It should uphold those traditions Christ set in place 2,000 years ago. As a woman I pray I don't see the day the Church condones female priests. "In persona Christi" rings strongly in my heart as indicative of the gender that needs to carry out such an incredible call and role in our Church.

I believe that the Catholic Church needs to maintain the strong foundation that it has since the time of St. Peter as our first pope. The moment that the Catholic Church begins to change and allow lay people to do more and/or allow women to become priests will be the fast downfall of the true Catholic Church. I fear that many Catholic churches are becoming too lenient and ignoring the basic teachings of the church. If we change to fit the selfish and liberal needs of our current society we will lose the authentic and genuine faith that has lasted for over 2000 years.

(4b) Accept married priests and women priests

I feel as though priests should be allowed to marry if they feel that they can handle such responsibilities. Many issues relating to this I feel are creating a shortage of good priests here and around the world. I think there are many, many married people around the world that possess the calling, but are unable to answer it.

The church should do away with stupid chastity laws. Other religions allow their priests and pastors to marry. What the heck is wrong with us? There is no reason to force someone to give up their sexuality for God. That is a gift and should be expressed sacredly in marriage.

I feel that the Church is unstable because of the sex scandals. I think allowing priests to marry would encourage more people to consider the priesthood and decrease the incidences of sexual abuse. If we can really trust our priests, the Church can move forward. With the present system, I'm not sure if it's possible to fully regain that trust, because nothing has really changed.

I think that the biggest challenge the Church is going to face in the years ahead is a lack of ordained priests. Personally, I feel that priests should be allowed to marry, and even that women should be able to be ordained. I know this breaks with thousands of years of tradition, but even Peter was married. Also, Jesus may have been a man, but he could not have been a woman and be taken seriously at that time. I am afraid that the Church needs to adapt if it is going to survive.

I think the biggest thing that needs to change is mandatory celibacy for priests. As long as priests can't marry, we will never solve the priest shortage problem. Family is such a huge emphasis in the Catholic tradition that I think most people are unwilling to give this up who might otherwise become priests. I think some orders of priests should maintain celibacy, but not everyone. It is known that celibacy is merely a tradition with no liturgical background.

Diocesan sample comments:

Catholics deserve the highest quality priests possible, and this is only possible if we draw from the entire population of our church—men and women, married or celibate. Such a change, while it might seem frightening to the leadership, would bring a tremendous sense of renewal to the Catholic Church. They need to act soon before it's too late.

In my town, we have six parishes. All have stable or growing membership, good to very good finances, we support four schools that are full, etc. And yet we are going to have to link and close parishes simply because we are running out of priests. In a sadly funny move, the diocese sent all of us on the Parish Council a 24-point questionnaire on "the viability of the parish." I felt like writing in crayon, "WE are doing fine. How are YOU doing? How about a few priests over here?" I didn't, of course. But we are not here to gently manage the decline of our faith; we are here to teach, act, and grow our faith. We are strangling ourselves by enforcing a ban on married priests.

Stop worrying who gets to wash the dishes and start making more priests! At this time of Eucharistic crisis, limiting the priesthood to celibate, heterosexual males is a ludicrous policy. The gifts of the married, of homosexuals, and of women should be employed on behalf of the assembly in the role of presider at the Eucharist. Sexual orientation and gender in no way inhibit the exercise of the presbyteral office.

I think we should be able to have women priests and that priests should be able to get married. I think God cares a lot more about the word of God being preached than about what gender you are. What qualities do males have that make them better priests? Also if priests could get married, this would not only decrease the shortage of priests, but priests could be looked on as people we could identify with more. If not being married somehow makes you any closer to God, then what does that say about the sacrament of marriage? I don't think we need to "throw the book out the window and start over" by any means, but times change and the Church should make some adjustments to account for this.

All of my research indicates that vocations are down. The Church, like any other institution or organization, needs to move with the economy, culture, etc. I cannot count the number of times that I have returned home from mass on Sunday, disheartened. It seems that our priests are aging, young priests are slow to follow, our parishes are saddled with debt, the collections don't cover the debts, and they speak of closing/consolidating churches and Catholic schools. These are beautiful churches and schools which have graced our community for decades. As a former student at a Catholic university, I've had numerous discussions about this. While we've disagreed on much, we've agreed on one thing: allow priests to marry.

After displaying these recommendations, we may note here that a 2005 Gallup poll asked Catholics whether or not they favor married men priests and women priests. The results were similar to the proportions favoring and disfavoring the ideas in our samples. In the nationwide sample, 74 percent of all Catholics eighteen to thirty-nine years old favored having married diocesan priests, 68 percent favored ordaining celibate women as priests, and 56 percent favored ordaining married women as priests (D'Antonio et al., 77). Apparently, our samples are voicing opinions widely held by young Catholics.

(5) Stressing love, forgiveness, and acceptance rather than strict rules

From the college students:

> In my opinion the Church should come down to the values which unite us, the most important being the love for our fellow human beings. We should have a distinction between these areas we can all celebrate and areas of our personal lives which are no one's business and responsibility but our own. The Church must without a doubt provide better support and acceptance for the GLBT among the congregation, not only for fear of losing their Catholic membership or to fit modern trends, but because it is the good Christian thing to do. And as much as I am pro-life, the Church must find that the basis for supporting pro-life stances cannot be limited to the Bible, but to an encompassing logic and reasoning. Otherwise we would just be preaching to the choir—literally.

The Church should stress the love and forgiveness that God has for us. I feel that too many Catholics are being turned off by the seemingly "strict" hand of the Church. While we must not forget or limit our traditions, we must also embody a more welcoming spirit and attitude, especially with those who feel estranged from the Church.

I feel that the Catholic Church should put a greater emphasis on the salvation that comes from Jesus Christ and less emphasis on Church laws. I feel that this would be in accordance with what Paul says in the book of Galatians, in that often people get so caught up with the many rules and laws that they forget that there is no amount of laws that we could follow that would make us closer to God. Only faith in Jesus and his salvation for us can absolve us in God's eyes.

The Church, like all Christians, needs to stress Christ's fundamental messages more: love one another, forgiveness, help the poor, etc. Too often people meet up with a "details" Catholic—someone who focuses all the time on doctrine and small details, and they are so distracted by this that they turn from the Church.

More churches need to stress the love of God for ALL of his people, not just Catholics who go to church every Sunday. There are many people in this world who feel the Church hates them, and in turn, God either doesn't exist for them or they are bitter toward the concept of his love.

We are all capable of love, and we are all children of God. We need to be more tolerant and accepting of others. We need to work on unity with each other no matter what race, ethnicity, gender, or sexual prefer-ence. We're all in this together, so why not start acting that way? In other words, LOVE is the answer. LOVE is where it's at. "And if I give all I possess to the poor and surrender my body to the flames, but have not love, I have nothing" (Corinthians 13:3).

The church should stress caring for its people, anti-war messages, and community. The Catholic Church would be such a strong force in the world if it didn't seem to succumb to its own rules. I feel that rules (in our diocese), like not holding hands during communion and not being allowed to have round churches, are petty. Really, the church should focus on teaching the children and the youth how to spread God's love in the community and to incorporate it in their lives. I love being Catholic but sometimes I have difficulties because Catholics have stereotypes built up against them due to never-changing habits which are misinterpreted by the world.

I am concerned about helping others and being active in the community, and I enjoy being with other people. The Church should stress these activities. We question so much these days and being fed rules (man-made) really pushes me and others away. For example, if we should love each other unconditionally, who cares if someone is homosexual? When I see some of my friends who are caring, good citizens doing God's work being told they are sinners because they love someone who is the same sex, it is just truly sad.

From the diocesan sample:

We need healing and bringing people back to the church, more acceptance of people where they are at—openness to people who have been divorced, also openness to gays and lesbians in the church.

I think it needs to focus on love a little more. To love those who sin, especially those who sin "publicly" such as being divorced, etc. I do not like how Christians are perceived as being almost hateful towards people who do not always follow Church teachings. None of us follow Church teachings perfectly, you just can't always tell. I do not, however, want the Church to water down teachings on sexuality, abortion, etc. The Church needs to be strong, but forgiving and loving.

The church should stress forgiveness. I know a few people who are divorced who were told they could no longer receive the sacrament of communion because of their divorce. Those people who need God the most should not be turned away. None of us are worthy to receive him, but turning those away due to divorce only turns people off from our faith. With our members dwindling and the Bible churches cropping up everywhere with huge churches and huge congregations, it is easy to see that the Catholic faith isn't flexible enough.

Move toward helping people live out their Catholic faith in a personal, spiritual way and as a beacon of God, rather than judgment.

Be welcome to accept ALL people, regardless of their sexual orientation, decision to have children, or the religion they are. All people should be welcome into the house of God without judgment! Why does one religion have to be right? Who said Catholics are better?

We need to be more open and accepting of all. Did not Christ associate with tax collectors and sinners? We need to move into the 21st century on issues of homosexuality, divorce, birth control.

We need to change the focus of the religion so that it is motivated by joy and not by guilt, teaching about sin but not living in constant flagellation over sin.

Concluding Reflections

We are adding a few of our own reflections and conclusions at the end of our report. They are modest. The role of Church-related research, such as the project we have carried out, is a limited one. Its purpose is to provide reliable information to Church leaders to help them make decisions.

To illustrate, recall the experience of walking into an airliner when boarding for a flight. To the left you can look into the cockpit and see dozens of dials and gauges, plus seats for the pilot and copilot. Our research is analogous to these dials and gauges in that it provides the information that the pilot needs. Research does not make decisions. The pilot alone makes all the decisions. For the Church, the pilot is the bishops and their advisors.

We believe that some facts about Catholic trends in America are beyond dispute. The number of Catholics is rising, while the number of priests is declining. Average size of parishes is rising and will continue to rise. Parishes are complex and expensive, and managing them is more than one priest or even two priests can do. They need professional lay staff, thus lay ministers will increase in importance in the years ahead.

The task of today's leadership is to carry out the Church's mission with human resources different from the resources we have had in the past. We need to recruit more priests, brothers, sisters, and lay ministers. More jobs need to be opened for lay ministers, and Catholic educational centers need to provide the training. Priests and lay ministers need to collaborate with each other.

The young generation of Catholics will produce enough candidates for the jobs if opportunities are opened. Lay ministry is widely felt to be a calling by God to serve the Church and the people. It is a meaningful, gratifying life.

The goal now should be to recruit and train the most talented and devoted lay ministers possible. Salaries need to be raised and institutional support of all kinds needs to be strengthened. It will be necessary to be in communication with seminaries and priest organizations to avoid misunderstandings and conflict.

We ran across three widespread cultural assumptions that will influence what is possible. Some Catholics seem to think that lay ministry is women's work—almost like the assumption that nursing is women's work. Also many seem to think

that young people in their twenties are suited for youth ministry and music ministry but not for other ministry jobs such as
pastoral associate. Finally, the diaconate is considered by most
to be for older men, not young men.

We got the impression from the responses to our surveys
that many of these young adults have already made life decisions that steered them away from future ministry. Apparently
we got to them too late. Had the Church leadership appealed
to them at an earlier age and more convincingly, more would
have seen ministry as a real option. This conclusion is rein-
forced by the insistence of our respondents that the Church
needs to give more energy and resources to youth ministry.
Nobody should assume that children of Catholic families will
automatically be good prospects for future ministry; rather,
we need to "recruit" them actively into life in the Church and
into ministry.

Young adults have important viewpoints about how to
strengthen the faith and the Catholic community. We have
summarized their suggestions. They are united in urging
more attention to youth and young adults, and in urging more
empowerment of lay people in parishes. On some topics they
are divided. But they need to be listened to.

Now we leave the implications of this research to others,
while urging goodwill and charity on all who are prayerfully
trying to discern the Church's way into the future.

Commentary:
Edward P. Hahnenberg

The most important thing about *The Next Generation of Pastoral Leaders* is not what questions were asked or what answers were given, but who was asked and who answered. As the authors clearly explain, this study is not a random sample of all Catholic youth. Rather it is a focused survey of two select groups: (1) Catholic college students active in campus ministry and (2) young adult Catholics who are not students, but who are known to their local dioceses. In other words, the study reports on the views and opinions of those young Catholics who are already (at least minimally) involved in the Church. It is a study of a slice of the Catholic youth population—a slice right off the top.

The select nature of the sample is the limitation of *The Next Generation*. But it is at the same time its distinct contribution, and its strength. In these pages, the authors introduce us to those young Catholics for whom the Church "works." These young adult Catholics are the ones who are involved. They are the ones who most likely will be involved. Thus they truly are the next generation of Catholic leaders. And the gift of this study it that allows their voices to be heard.[1]

Much of what these young Catholics say is encouraging. Many of them have given significant thought to a life of ministry. Over half of the men surveyed said they had seriously considered becoming a priest. More than a third of all respondents—men and women—expressed an interest in professional lay ministry. Overwhelmingly, these young Catholics understand ministry as a response to a call from God and an opportunity to help other people. They are aware of the need to discern their individual gifts in light of the needs of the community.

But there is also cause for concern in this study. Despite all the interest in lay ministry, very few young adults end up choosing it as a vocation. What keeps them from wanting to work for the Church? For the idealistic college students, the number-one reason is "I have a different occupation in mind." For the world-wise college grads, it is low wages, long hours, and lack of job security that loom larger. No doubt these obstacles to entering ministry will draw the attention of Church leaders. Here are concrete issues to take up and grapple with as a Church. Further direction is given when the authors of the study invite young adult lay ministers to offer their own recommendations. They ask of their bishop: (1) better appreciation and support, (2) more opportunities for spiritual development, (3) more financial support, and (4) more credentialing. These obstacles and these ideas suggest a healthy and heavy agenda for strengthening the future of pastoral leadership. They give us an excellent place to start. But this study also invites us to reflect on the larger opportunities and challenges facing this new generation of American Catholics.

This Generation

The introductory chapter of *The Next Generation* describes the present lifestage of twenty- and thirty-somethings in the United States as "emerging adulthood." This is where most of the respondents in this survey find themselves in their own life story—in a somewhat extended transitional period between adolescence and adulthood. "Emerging adulthood" is a relatively new stage of life in our culture, and it deserves attention for the ways in which it shapes the process of vocational discernment. But to fully understand this group of young Catholics, it is important to look not only at their age, but also at their generation.

Age affects how we look at things. Children tend to be accepting and imaginative. Adolescents often strive for self-expression. Adults typically grow more comfortable with ambiguity. But one's age is different from one's generation. Different generations can be identified because historical events hit groups of people in a particular society at different ages. The "Baby Boomers" are no longer eighteen years old. But they share a generational identity because of what they experienced together when they were eighteen. Now at sixty, they see the world differently than did their parents or their grandparents at sixty.

In their important longitudinal study *American Catholics Today*, William D'Antonio and his colleagues identify three main generations comprising the Catholic Church in the United States: pre-Vatican II Catholics (born before 1941), Vatican II Catholics (born 1941-1960), and post-Vatican II Catholics (born after 1961).[2] These three Catholic categories—keyed to the event of the Second Vatican Council—roughly correspond to the categories used by secular sociologists: the "Greatest Generation," "Baby Boomers," and "Generation X"/"Millennials." The differences between these generations offer a helpful perspective on the attitudes toward Church and ministry reported in this study, thus it is worth reflecting on the broad characteristics of each.

Pre-Vatican II Catholics experienced the effects of the Great Depression and World War II. They grew up in the largely immigrant Church of the 1940s and 1950s, a world in which many Catholics were relegated to the fringes of American society. Their way of being Catholic in a Protestant country was to build up a world of their own. National parishes supported the construction of parallel institutions (Catholic schools, hospitals, orphanages, and credit unions) and fostered a distinctive religious subculture (Mass in Latin, meatless Fridays, novenas, holy hours, and Marian devotions) that set pre-Vatican II Catholics apart from the rest of American society.

The next generation, the Vatican II Catholics, lived through the dissolution of this distinctive American Catholic subculture, a sociological shift that had as much to do with World War II as it did with Vatican II. They are the Baby Boomer generation, that large bulge in the American population created by the unusually high birth rates following the war. Baby Boomer Catholics grew up in the tranquility of the 1950s and were shaped by the shockwaves of the 1960s. In high school and college, the Boomers fueled antiwar protests, joined the women's movement, and fought for civil rights. But alongside this very vocal social protest was a more quiet social accommodation. These Vatican II Catholics reaped the benefits of the rising affluence of their parents. The G.I. Bill had opened up college education to the sons of working immigrants. As Catholics got richer, they moved out of ethnic neighborhoods and into the suburbs. And as Catholics integrated into American society, the Catholic subculture started to fade. For many Vatican II Catholics, the Council symbolized the new freedom that came with leaving the Catholic ghetto and engaging the modern world.

Very different experiences have shaped post-Vatican II Catholics, a generation that is comprised of two groups. Sociologists call the older cohort Generation X and point out that this group came of age in a much less idealistic time than did either their parents or grandparents. This is a generation of Americans raised in the world of divorce and fragmented families, a group that grew up under the looming threat of the Cold War and the ballooning deficits of the Reagan years. The distrust of institutions that fed the protests of the Baby Boomers has developed into open cynicism and a certain apathy among many Gen-Xers. They watched African famines on television, witnessed the rise of AIDS, saw environmental disaster after disaster, and still find themselves facing a host of problems that it seems previous generations have handed on. The response of some has been advocacy; for many it has meant withdrawal. But recent studies have identified a post-Generation X cohort, called "Generation Y" or "Millennials." This group (born after 1980) seems to carry the characteristics of a more confident, idealistic, and socially conscious generation—perhaps shifting the balance toward greater engagement in politics and greater commitment to social concerns.[3]

Despite their differences, both Generation X and Millennials share many of the same attitudes toward religion and Church. These post-Vatican II Catholics did not experience the closed Catholic subculture of the past, they never knew the enthusiasm of the Council, and they have little familiarity with the Church today. They have a weak connection to institutional

Catholicism. They consider themselves Catholic, and they like being Catholic, but they want to do it on their own terms. What they have experienced of the Church has mostly been the Church's encouragement for them to take responsibility for their own faith journey. Thus they tend to be more individualistic and eclectic, "spiritual, but not religious." Many of the Church's structures, policies, and rules do not make much sense to them (Why can't women be priests? What's wrong with homosexuality?). Any appeal to authority or any exclusive claim to truth grates against the values of diversity, tolerance, and acceptance that is the air these young adults breathe. If the story of the pre-Vatican II generation over the past forty years has been a story of loss, and that of Vatican II Catholics a story of liberation, then the story of this post-Vatican II generation is a story of lack. It is a story of little religious knowledge, low institutional commitment, and less and less involvement in the life of the Church.

If this characterization of post-Vatican II Catholics is correct, then it only underlines the exceptional nature of the young adults surveyed in *The Next Generation*. Indeed, one of the things that sets apart the respondents to this study from the vast majority of their peers is that their names made it onto a Church list somewhere, a list that allowed them to be contacted in the first place. But by "exceptional," I am not making a claim about the depth of their faith relative to their peers. Indeed, there is much that is positive and good in the religious attitudes of the broader post-Vatican II generation: attention to a personal relationship with God, a sense of ownership of their spiritual journey, an ecumenical sensitivity and appreciation for dialogue. To speak of the lack of post-Vatican II Catholics is not to imply an emptiness inside these young adults. Rather, it is to recognize a lack of connection between them and their Catholicism. That is where the respondents are exceptional: the respondents are connected, they are involved—even if only minimally—in the Church.

Implications

If there is a single finding that summarizes this study, it is this: those young adults who are active in the Church find it easier to imagine staying active. So if our goal is to promote the Church leadership of tomorrow, we ought to be asking how we foster Church involvement today. If half of all young adults who are active in the Church have seriously considered entering full-time ministry, my question is this: How do we get more young adults to be active? Three thoughts flow out of this study.

1. Place Choice in the Context of Call. College-educated American Catholics face an almost overwhelming number of options. Raised to believe that they can be anything they want to be and conditioned daily by our advertising culture, young adults instinctively think of a career on the model of consumer choice. I get to pick. (It is not insignificant that, in the survey, the number-one reason given for not pursuing a life of ministry—outweighing even celibacy for the priesthood—is that the respondent had a different career in mind.) This consumer mentality extends beyond career to influence how many young people understand their values, their lifestyle, and even their faith.

Perhaps one reason so many young Catholics have a weak connection to the Church, and thus are less involved and active, is that the Church itself has become a commodity. It is one other thing that I can choose to include in my life. Within such a consumer mentality, faith becomes radically diluted. Faith is less than faith when it is simply one part of life, rather than that which orients all of life. While the model of choice has its strengths (an emphasis on agency and intentionality, for example), it needs to be placed in the context of God's call. We need a better theology of vocation to show how the spiritual search—so strong among the young—always comes as a response to the loving invitation and uncomfortable challenge that is the call of God.

2. Affirm Identity through Engagement. The authors note a divide between those young adults who want the Church to "go back to tradition" and those who want the Church to "relate more to modern life" (with the latter far outnumbering the former). Typically, this is cast as a divide between those who want to preserve religious identity and those who want to promote religious engagement. The authors point out that the youth who advocate change are not advocating change in the core teachings of Catholicism. When we read the words of these young adults, we hear a call for more dynamic liturgies, better music, relevant messages, less guilt, and more flexibility—not a radical rejection or basic dismissal of the faith. In the same way, those young adults who want to return to tradition are also concerned more with the periphery than with the core of Church teaching. Rather than lively liturgies, they emphasize reverence at Mass, celibacy for priests, and the need for conservative practices like adoration and the use of Latin.

It seems to me that this is less a divide between identity and engagement than it is a glimpse into different sensibilities about how to practice the faith today. In these scattered suggestions, we see an uncertainty about how to "do" Catholicism. This should not surprise us. Given our consumer culture, many young Catholics have developed a good sense of themselves as active agents of their personal beliefs. They recognize that they have a responsibility to shape their own personal spirituality or life philosophy, and they take this responsibility seriously. But what many of them do not have is a sense of themselves as active agents of their religious tradition. They see themselves as recipients, or beneficiaries, of the faith, but not as active contributors to it. Why? Because in a thousand little ways, they have been socialized into passivity. In the end, all the attention Church leaders have given to Catholic identity in recent years—as important as it is—seems wasted if it is not an identity built on drawing Catholics of all ages into full, conscious, and active participation in the life of the Church.

3. Strengthen Ministry for Mission.   One of the most troubling things about *The Next Generation* is how little attention the respondents give to issues of outreach, mission, and social justice. This may simply follow from the fact that the questions in the survey ask about lay ministry, religious life, and the priesthood—which are typically seen as ministries directed toward the inner life of the Church. But it raises a question for those who work with young adults. Is there a disconnect between the motivations charted in this study and the motivations of the thousands of young Catholics who engage in service outside the Church? How do the few college students who are seriously considering lay ecclesial ministry relate to their many peers who have never considered that possibility, but who sign up for urban plunge weekends, alternative spring breaks, and even year-long service programs? In other words, have we compartmentalized ministry, cordoning it off from mission? Have we suggested to our youth that the choice is between service in the Church or service to the world?

Clearly, Catholic Christians find many ways to serve the reign of God. But I wonder if we haven't separated things more than they need to be. How might the future of Church leadership be strengthened if we brought out more clearly the profound links between ministry and mission? How many more young people might we inspire if we learn to talk about and act like the ministry that serves the Church community serves that community precisely in order to strengthen it for its mission in the world? This may be one of the most important questions among the many important questions raised by *The Next Generation of Pastoral Leaders*.

Edward P. Hahnenberg *is the author of* Ministries: A Relational Approach *(Crossroad) and* A Concise Guide to the Documents of Vatican II *(St. Anthony Messenger Press). A past consultant to the U.S. Bishops' Subcommittee on Lay Ministry, he teaches theology at Xavier University in Cincinnati, Ohio.*

---

1. Other recent studies to be read alongside *The Next Generation* include Dean R. Hoge, William D. Dinges, Mary Johnson, and Juan L. Gonzales, Jr., *Young Adult Catholics: Religion in the Culture of Choice* (Notre Dame, IN: University of Notre Dame Press, 2001); Christian Smith and Melinda Lundquist Denton, *Soul Searching: The Religious and Spiritual Lives of American Teenagers* (Oxford: Oxford University Press, 2005); "The Spiritual Life of College Students: A National Study of Students' Search for Meaning and Purpose," a report of a multiyear study on spirituality

in higher education conducted by the Higher Education Research Institute at UCLA (www.spirituality.ucla.edu); David DeLambo, *Lay Parish Ministers: A Study of Emerging Leadership* (New York: National Pastoral Life Center, 2005); Dean R. Hoge, *The First Five Years of Priesthood: A Study of Newly Ordained Catholic Priests* (Collegeville, MN: Liturgical Press, 2002). An accessible introduction is Thomas P. Rausch, *Being Catholic in a Culture of Choice* (Collegeville, MN: Liturgical Press, 2006).

2. William V. D'Antonio, James D. Davidson, Dean R. Hoge, and Mary L. Gautier, *American Catholics Today: New Realities of Their Faith and Their Church* (Lanham, MD: Sheed & Ward, 2007). In this latest study—a follow-up to studies in 1987, 1993, and 1999—the authors introduce a fourth category, "Millennials," born 1979–1987. They acknowledge that the sample of this new group is small and warn that their findings on the Millennials should be interpreted with caution.

3. Neil Howe and William Straus, *Millennials Rising: The Next Great Generation* (New York: Vintage Books, 2000).

Commentary:
Rachel Hart Winter

I hope you come to find that which gives life a deep meaning for you. Something worth living for—maybe even worth dying for—something that energizes you, enthuses you, enables you to keep moving ahead. I can't tell you what it might be—that's for you to find, to choose, to love. I can just encourage you to start looking, and to support you in your search.—Sr. Ita Ford, M.M. (Ford, Letter)

What are young adults looking for in the Church?

We are seeking community and loving relationships, meaning and a sense of vocation in our lives, and a place to sustain and nurture our faith.

Three years ago, I stood on the road where Ita Ford was killed. I was profoundly affected by the story of Ita, a Maryknoll sister working in El Salvador, and the three women who were murdered with her as a result of their commitment to justice for the people of El Salvador. Ita wrote the lines above in a letter to her niece shortly before her death. It still sends shivers down my spine when I read it and reflect on her faith and courage. I remember standing in awe, on the road where her life tragically ended, contemplating Ita's strong sense of vocation and commitment. I wondered what it must have felt like to have such a robust faith in God and such a concrete sense of vocation. Her words about finding meaning get to the heart of the desire I see in young adults today. Our lives move so quickly; we are constantly bombarded by noise; and we move between jobs, relationships, and commitments. Sometimes it is hard to know what the true meaning of our lives is. This is precisely where the Church can and should respond to the needs of young adults. The Church offers us a connection to the greatest meaning in our lives, our relationship with God.

As a thirty-one-year-old Catholic woman, I realize that I am extremely fortunate to remain active in my faith. I also feel gratitude to have great connections to a vibrant Catholic community in my life today. My experiences and work within the Church have constantly nourished and developed my faith. I was raised in a family where our faith was central. Sundays were not only the days that we went to Church, but also the day that we set aside time for family. I remember loving those days and knowing that they were special. I attended Sacred Heart High School, which integrated service and justice with my understanding of faith.

The most significant piece of my formation as a young adult was certainly my time as a volunteer with Jesuit Volunteers International (JVI). I served in the Republic of the Marshall Islands for two years as a sixth-grade teacher at a Catholic school. The pillars of the Jesuit Volunteers are simplicity, faith, community, and service. The challenge provided through the experience for me was matched by the joy and gratitude for the people I met and grew to love in the Islands. Prayer was not simply a requirement, but proved to be the glue for my own journey as well as that of my community. As volunteers we worked alongside the priests there and supported the mission of the school. I am certain that this experience has provided me with the necessary tools to work as a lay minister and to collaborate with both lay and ordained colleagues. This experience enabled me to articulate my need for community, a sense of vocation, and desire for faith. I discuss these ideas from my own experience before offering suggestions for ways the Church might provide these things for young adults.

Community

I will never forget the fear and excitement of receiving my placement with JVI, on a small island about which I knew nothing. On top of that, I was assigned to be a teacher, an occupation with which I had no experience. Luckily, I did not embark on this journey alone; I was gifted with a community that illuminated each step of the way. This group of peers and mentors helped me continually discover my own vocation in the Church. Community has existed in many forms for me, from my family to my volunteer community, to a faith-sharing group that I have been a member of for the last five years in Chicago. I know that I would not be where I am today if it were not for the people who have guided me on my journey and helped me understand my own vocation. Countless individuals have patiently walked with me, and that companionship is the gift I hope to share with young adults in my ministry as a chaplain at Loyola University Chicago.

Vocation

My family, mentors, and peers embody God's love for me and open my eyes to the things that I desire in my own life. These relationships keep me rooted in gratitude. All life is a gift: the ability to find God in all things, the desire to look with the eyes of Christ upon the world, and the conviction to stand for justice in any way possible, all with a reverent, contemplative attitude is my desire.

My experience of working for the Church as a volunteer led me to reflect honestly on what I wanted to do with my life and how I felt called to serve the world and the Church. It sparked my shift from premedical studies in college to a life focused on ministry and service within the Church. It also inspired me to pursue a doctoral degree in Christian ethics at Loyola University. Through both my field work as a chaplain and my studies in the classroom, I have discerned a calling to bring together academic study and the lived experience of faith so that one may illuminate the other.

Faith

We do not find the rewards of our faith and service in material goods; instead, we discover them in relationships and through an awareness of God in our lives. I am supported by community in my work as a chaplain, which sustains each of us in the work we do. I am also surrounded by peers that encourage me to pray, reflect, and stay connected to God in my life. Many of my professional choices in life are made out of a desire to grow in my faith. I was struck by the survey results of respondents who said that they would not consider ministry as a career option due to the salary. The work that I do each day offers such a great sense of purpose and gratitude that I feel few other careers offer. Ministry is certainly a vocation, but it is also something that we are all called to whether professionally or not. Ministry is connected to service. We are called to be servants and have the vocation of carrying this mission into all of our actions.

One of the greatest gifts for me in my work has been to share with students the joys of working for the Church. Each year I have accompanied various students who go on to further training in ministry. I believe invitations to young adults can open their eyes to ministry and the needs of the Church. It is amazing to watch young adults learn about the options available in the Church for both ordained and lay leadership. It is our job as professional ministers in the Church to invite young adults in and to offer creative ways to keep them involved.

What does the Church need to do to attract young people?

It is clear from the research that young people in the Church today have unique and different hopes and desires for their expectations of the Church. As I have come to learn more about the Church, that seems to be its beauty. The Church is a place where all are welcome, all are heard, and all should feel at home. One of the most important things I desire to see in the Church is more space for dialogue. The research reveals that there are several ways to view how the Church should function and what the Church leadership should look like. Instead of fostering an "us and them" attitude among its members, the Church ought to encourage dialogue so that all may understand the Church not as "mine" or "yours," but as "ours." We must help the entire community grow in embracing our call as "many parts" and "one body." Young people are not attracted to a Church where members feel hostility toward one another.

The Church should invite young adults by offering what we seek: community, vocation, and faith. I have felt empowered by the leaders in the Church who have aided in my formation and valued the contributions that I have to offer. This, then, is my goal: to empower the college students I work with and to encourage them to understand that they are the future of the Church and the great responsibility that accompanies that mission.

It is up to all of us to bring about God's vision of justice and peace for the world. We have a lot of work to do, and young adults are eager to join the work.

Below I offer brief ideas on the three areas of community, vocation, and faith for the Church to invigorate young adults.

The Church should be a place where young adults are able to find community. Some resources I have taken advantage of are Theology-on-Tap, retreats, book groups, and young-adult liturgies. These were places I turned when I was in my twenties and searching for a place to connect with others similar to myself. The Church will do well to continue to mine these areas that attract young adults, while continuing to creatively imagine new ways to meet young adults where they are and offer what they are seeking in terms of community and relationships. Another part of community is the intentional relationships that support us. So many have cared for me and loved me into the person I am today. Perhaps an idea would be to connect young adults with people ten or so years older to meet with them and journey together. Service opportunities and immersion experiences are also a great way for the Church to foster community around a shared experience.

The Church has more resources than any institution I can think of in terms of aiding young adults on their search for a sense of identity and vocation in life. These tools need to be used and celebrated. Dust off the old manuals of the lives of saints and allow young adults to connect with the great minds of people like Teresa of Ávila, Catherine of Siena, and Ignatius of Loyola. These people have been guides for me in my own search. Nothing is quite so profound as facing a challenge in my life today aware that others hundreds of years ago struggled with the same issues and used faith as a guide. Resources that have worked for me in the area of vocations have been seeing a spiritual director for the last ten years to help me continually discern God's will for me. Days of prayer and workshops on vocations have also aided me. Again, these resources should be proclaimed widely for young adults. When I tell college students about the opportunity to meet with a spiritual director, they welcome the chance to share with another about their relationship with God.

Finally, and perhaps most importantly, the Church has a great opportunity to accompany young adults on their journey through the work to strengthen and sustain our lives of faith. After completing my service as a volunteer, I participated in the Ignatian Spiritual Exercises. The retreat occurred over the course of a year where I prayed daily and met with a director once a week. This retreat encouraged me to incorporate prayer into my daily life. The effects of this have been numerous. Another area for the Church to invite young adults to grow is through an invitation to participate in the liturgy. Dynamic liturgies have the ability to transform our lives and teach people about the riches of our faith.

I have offered a few reflections from my own experience of a young adult along with the need that I discern as I accompany others on their journey of faith. Just as Sr. Ita Ford encouraged her niece to find meaning in her life, the Church ought to do the same by inviting its members to an ever-deepening life with each other and with God. The Church is in transition and although change can be hard, it is also precisely where hope and new opportunities for growth are found. Young adults have much to offer, and the Church has many gifts to share to meet the needs of youth today.

Rachel Winter works at Loyola University Chicago's Hank Center for the Catholic Intellectual Heritage. She is completing her doctorate in theology at Loyola where she has also worked as chaplain in ministry.

Commentary:
Paul E. Jarzembowski

The future is already here, but has anyone really noticed?

The Next Generation of Pastoral Leaders gives us a snapshot of that future by posing a variety of questions to active Catholic young adults in their twenties and thirties today.

As a diocesan leader of young adults, I know well and work with young adults just like the ones featured in this study. They are the dedicated men and women planning Theology-on-Tap programs, organizing young adult retreats, singing in their parish's choir on Sunday, or volunteering at local shelters and soup kitchens.

As I read through this study, what struck me was just how many of these people have seriously considered a role in Church leadership as a priest, deacon, religious brother or sister, or as a lay ecclesial minister like myself. I would guess that this stems from the taste of leadership given to them on their campus or in their local parish, or being around passionate and enthusiastic priests, sisters, and lay ministers.

On the other hand, this study also showed that while interest in Church leadership was high, the reality is much more sobering. The reality is that parishes and dioceses today employ few young people, and only a small number under forty are studying for ministry in seminaries or graduate schools. Furthermore, I have to wonder what leadership opportunities lay beyond the young adult retreat or the registration table of the local Theology-on-Tap. Would those active in young adult ministry find a home in the leadership of their local parish community? Would they find a place on a parish pastoral or finance council? Would they be allowed to add their creativity and ingenuity to the liturgical and ministerial life of their local parish?

Additionally, young adult ministers like myself are trained to ask yet another troublesome question: "Who's not here?" It's this evangelistic question that drives young adult ministers to keep reaching out beyond our comfort zone to find the twenty- and thirty-somethings disconnected, frustrated, or simply detached from the life of the Church. In this particular study, those who were interviewed and polled were those active young adult Catholics who are known to their pastors, campus ministers, or young adult ministers in one way or another. I kept wondering what young adult Catholics who are disconnected to these parishes and dioceses might say to the same questions, or how the people who are somewhat involved (but whose lives were too busy to answer questions like these) might respond to these issues.

And even more so, what about the millions of young adults who aren't even being reached because there is no place for them to connect? As the executive director of the National Catholic Young Adult Ministry Association, I can tell you with a sad certainty that there are less and less young adult ministry programs out there every year, and even fewer professional young adult ministers in our parishes and dioceses. That means that the number of young adults getting excited about Church leadership (like several of the people interviewed in *Next Generation*) is declining. It's not that young adults are turned off to working for the Church; rather, it's that there are less young adults being ministered to today, thereby shrinking the potential pool of future ministers.

Another important concern that is raised here is the image of a pastoral ministry career, from the perspective of Baby Boomers, Gen Xers, and Millennials alike. When asked what factors would be important to becoming a lay, vowed, or ordained minister, what was noticeably missing from the list was "It is a career I want to pursue." And perhaps this oversight might be a key factor to why a high number of respondents said that having a different occupation in mind was a major reason for their decision not to pursue Church work. If we do not present Church ministry as a potential career option amongst many, why are we so surprised that the young adults never really saw it that way to begin with? So when compared to all the other career opportunities laid out before collegians and young adults, pastoral ministry in the Church just doesn't register.

So what can be done? Here are a few recommendations, based on this data:

Develop intentional young adult ministry programs. If the strongest interest in Church ministry emerges from those who are actively involved in campus and young adult ministry, then put capital and resources into expanding those programs in parishes, campuses, and dioceses around the country. Those young adults who are being reached are just the tip of the iceberg, but unless more attention is given to this ministry, that ice, too, will melt. Even the active young adults in the study know their peers are missing, and in their recommendations for the Church, they clearly voiced their desire to expand young adult ministry outreach so that others can connect as they have.

Furthermore, if this is the ground floor upon which most pastoral leaders will springboard, why not have more opportunities like those given in active young adult and campus ministries? This will involve putting money and time toward hiring young adult ministry professionals, encouraging extensive programming for college students, singles, and young couples, and inviting those participants to take a more active role in their faith lives (rather than seeing themselves as "participants" and "attendees").

Make room for young adults in parish leadership. The young adults in the *Next Generation* study might be involved with young adult ministry efforts on their campuses or parishes, but what a blessing it would be to invite them into the leadership of their local parish communities. Men and women in their twenties and thirties ought to be actively recruited for seats on pastoral councils or finance boards and active leadership roles in liturgical ministries, or given the opportunity to develop new or grow existing ministries in their parishes. All it takes is a simple, personal, and verbal invitation from an authority in the Church community. I can only imagine what might happen if those who had such strong opinions in this study would be invited into active leadership in their local Church.

This would not only give energy and new blood to the parish, but it would also give young adults the chance to work closely with the Church and develop their ministry leadership skills. About a quarter of the young adults surveyed claimed that lay or ordained ministry did not utilize their gifts and talents, so this experience might offer them a new perspective to that assumption. If young adults are willing to step into the role of leader in a campus or young adult ministry setting, a personal invitation to leadership in a local parish community just might yield even greater response to future ministry.

Finally, this study calls on the Church to adopt a new culture of vocations and a greater sense of cooperation and synergy between ministries. We simply cannot operate in separate worlds anymore. Those who work in ministries dedicated to increasing vocations, developing lay ecclesial ministers, and organizing the diaconate program need to work hand-in-hand with those who minister to college students and young adults in the diocese and in the parish.

On a national level, we have seen great success from the partnerships that religious communities have had when they get involved with young adult ministry. Three major examples of this are the Paulist Fathers in New York City, who founded Busted Halo Ministries (www.bustedhalo.com), known especially for their incredibly interactive Web site for spiritual seekers, as well as their podcast, radio show, blogs, question boxes, Church search, and retreats; the Jesuits of the Chicago Province, who created Charis Ministries (www .charisministries.org), which developed a series of young adult retreats and days of prayer, now held around the country and all based on the Spiritual Exercises of St. Ignatius of Loyola; and the many local priests, deacons, and lay ministers who are actively supporting and shepherding the work of Spirit & Truth (www.sandt.org), an organized nationwide network of Eucharistic adoration communities begun in Atlanta and now flourishing in parishes, campuses, and dioceses from coast to coast.

What this does is shift the paradigm to the way young adults "do Church" now in the twenty-first century. In decades past, vocations to lay, vowed, or ordained ministry would result from introducing young people to inspirational Church ministers in their local parish communities. But due to the clergy shortage and the busyness of life for many families, there are fewer opportunities for this kind of experience. However, when lay and diaconate formation directors and vocation coordinators for ordained and vowed communities cooperate alongside youth, campus, and young adult ministries, we might be able to regain and reclaim a new culture of vocations. The national organizations for youth ministry, campus ministry, and young adult ministry are already working harder to collaborate more effectively so that young people can walk a seamless road from one experience of Church to the next (instead of falling through the gaps between our ministry areas). Ideally we would keep that bridge continuing beyond young adulthood into a life of service and ministry in the Church. We can no longer live in the age of isolation; we must work together to help and support each other's good work.

So in addition to "praying for vocations" at Mass today, we can now add a new step: work at developing active campus and young adult ministries in our parishes and diocese where those vocations can take root.

As someone who works with young adults, I can firmly state that the future isn't just beyond the next decade; rather, it's right here in front of us. The "next generation" in the title of this book isn't coming one day, it's already here. But there are three important questions I want to pose to those of us already involved in Church work. One, do we have good outreach ministries in place for collegians and young adults? Two, are we actively recruiting and offering invitations to young Catholics to greater leadership opportunities? And three, can we start thinking in new and creative ways to broaden our outreach and work hand-in-hand with one another?

If you need proof of this need, just read through the final section of *The Next Generation*. The young adults interviewed are begging for more, but is anyone listening?

Paul Jarzembowski is the Executive Director of the National Catholic Young Adult Ministry Association and full-time Director of Young Adults Ministry in the Diocese of Joliet in Illinois.

Appendix: Research Methods

The College Student Survey

Beginning in December 2006 we contacted Catholic campus ministries in a random sample of twenty colleges and universities throughout the nation. They included Catholic, private, and public institutions, in proportionate numbers. We asked them to forward our online survey to a random sample of all the students known to them, not just to their regular participants or leadership circle. We wanted the most representative sample possible of all Catholic students on the campus.

We set the nationwide sample at one thousand and calculated how many should be sent out at each institution, depending on size, with a maximum of one hundred. On average, the online survey went to about fifty students per campus, with a range of twelve at the smallest college to one hundred at the largest. Respondents had a choice of an English or a Spanish version.

We paid all campus ministries for their participation. We asked the campus ministers to send out the survey twice within a three-week interval, beginning at the end of February 2007. Although twenty agreed to participate, one did not. Thus the total surveys forwarded to e-mail addresses was 914. By April we had 434 completions in English and five in Spanish, for a total of 439. We deleted anyone not a student and anyone over thirty-nine years of age (a total of eighteen), thus the total number of completions was 421, or 47 percent.

The colleges were SUNY. at Oneonta, St. Joseph's in Philadelphia, East Carolina University, University of North Carolina–Charlotte, Mississippi University for Women, University of Southern Mississippi, University of Notre Dame, Indiana University–South Bend, University of Illinois–Champaign, Illinois State University–Normal, Illinois Wesleyan University, Fort Hayes State University, Kansas State University–Manhattan, University of Texas–El Paso, University of Texas–Permian Basin, California State University–Long Beach, University of Southern California, Oregon State University–Corvallis, and University of Portland.

Survey of Young Adults from Diocesan Lists

To collect attitudes of nonstudents, we contacted a random sample of thirteen dioceses nationwide, one for each apostolic region, and asked if they could assemble an e-mail list of young adults twenty to thirty-nine years of age. We paid them for their help. We aimed for a sample of twelve hundred, and we calculated how many should be sent out in each diocese. The maximum was 114.

Not all the dioceses could participate, since some had no lists to work from. Thus we made four substitutions, in each case going to a neighboring diocese. In California we needed to divide the sample into two dioceses because of the large number of persons needed. Of the fourteen dioceses who agreed, two did not participate in the end, reducing our sample to twelve. They were Hartford; New York; Altoona-Johnstown; St. Petersburg; Cincinnati; Green Bay; Bismarck; Wichita; San Angelo; San Jose; San Diego; and Yakima.

Not every diocese followed our directions. Two dioceses sent out more than we specified, so our best estimate is that about 1235 were actually forwarded. By May, we received 732 completed English responses and thirty Spanish. We deleted anyone not Catholic and anyone too young or old (nineteen or younger, or forty or older), leaving 701 suitable respondents, for a response rate of about 65 percent.

To avoid overlap with the college student survey, we deleted everyone currently a college student (233 cases), leaving 468 persons not currently college students.

We are unclear exactly who were on the samples compiled by the dioceses, so the survey of young adults is less than precisely describable. Whereas we know how the campus ministers constructed their lists, we do not know the same for the diocesan staff. All we know is that the diocesan sample includes persons quite active in Catholic parishes and programs.

Respondents in the 2007 Surveys

Table A.1 tells us who are in the two samples. The clear majority in both were women. Most of the college students were twenty to twenty-nine years old, although some were younger. Of the diocesan sample, half were twenty to twenty-nine and half were thirty to thirty-nine. The students averaged about twenty-three years old and the nonstudents about twenty-nine. The college students were roughly divided between freshmen, sophomores, juniors, and seniors, plus a few graduate students. In the college sample, 13 percent considered themselves to be Hispanic or Latino/a.

Table A.1
Characteristics of Sample Members (in percents)

	Student Sample		Diocesan Sample	
	Males	Females	Males	Females
Number of Cases:	(173)	(247)	(157)	(287)
Age: 18 or 19	27	30	0	0
20 to 29	70	69	55	53
30 to 39	3	1	45	47
Do you consider yourself to be Hispanic or Latino/a?				
Yes	13	13	10	9
No	87	87	90	91
Were you born in the USA?				
Yes	94	93	93	94
No	6	7	7	6
In what year of college are you—a freshman, sophomore, junior, senior, or graduate student?				
Freshman	19	17		
Sophomore	23	27		
Junior	25	26		
Senior	24	25		
Graduate student	10	5		
In the last six months, have you been involved in any Catholic campus groups for worship, service, or socializing?				
Yes, an officer or leader	26	24		
Yes, a participant	54	50		
Yes, at least one event	9	10		
Yes, an employee	1	0		
No	10	15		
(if not a student:) Have you ever attended college?				
Yes, some college			16	17
Yes, a four-year degree			54	50
Yes, a graduate degree			26	30
No			4	3

As Table A.1 shows, most of the college students have participated to some extent in a Catholic campus ministry program. Only 10 percent of the men and 15 percent of the women have not done so; their names got onto campus ministry lists somehow even though they never participated. About one-fourth were officers or leaders in the campus group, and about half were participants but not leaders.

We asked the college students if they have ever volunteered in a service organization for a week or more. Thirty-eight percent of the men and 30 percent of the women said yes. We also asked them if they are currently studying religion, theology, philosophy, or sacred music. Only 4 percent said it was their major. The majority, 70 percent, said no.

Turning to the diocesan sample, almost all the people have attended college, 96 percent of the men and 95 percent of the women. Further, 25 percent of the men and 29 percent of the women have graduate degrees. We could, in effect, name the diocesan sample the "active college alumni sample." In this sample, 9 percent said they were Hispanic or Latino/a.

Personal Interviews and Focus Groups

The fifty-five personal interviews were done in four geographical areas. Getting a random sample of persons was impossible, but we included a variety of young adult Catholics, both parish-involved and not involved. Half the interviews were in person and half were by phone. Fifteen interviews were with persons working full-time as lay ministers. All the interviews were taped and transcribed. The four focus groups were done in different locations, involving a variety of young Catholic

Table A.2
Differences Between Latinos and Non-Latinos (in percents)

	Student Sample		Diocesan Sample	
	Latinos	Others	Latinos	Others
Number of cases:	(54)	(364)	(42)	(400)
Were you born in the USA? ("yes")	81	95	67	96
Have you ever attended college? ("yes, four-year degree or more")			43	84
Have you ever seriously considered becoming a professional lay minister, such as director of religious education, youth minister, campus minister, music minister, or pastoral associate? ("yes")	39	34	71	50

Here are reasons people sometimes give for not being interested in serving as a lay minister. Whether or not you are personally interested, how influential would each of these factors be in discouraging you? ("very influential")

I have a different occupation in mind	45	63	22	40
It does not utilize my gifts and talents	12	24	27	34
It is only short-term, with no long-term future	13	15	32	23
Too much education is required	0	5	17	6
I know too little about it to be interested	19	12	17	8
Has anyone ever encouraged you to consider ministry as a priest, brother, or sister? ("yes")	39	49	60	49

Here are reasons sometimes given for interest in becoming a priest, sister, or brother. Whether or not you are personally interested, how important would each be to you? ("very important")

It is an opportunity to provide the Sacraments	44	42	65	47
It is an opportunity to preach God's Word	54	62	81	63
It utilizes my gifts and talents	60	53	76	62

Table A.2 *continued*

Differences Between Latinos and Non-Latinos (in percents)

Here are reasons sometimes given for not becoming a priest, sister, or brother. How influential would each be in discouraging you, whether or not you are personally interested? ("very influential")

	Student Sample		Diocesan Sample	
	Latinos	Others	Latinos	Others
Number of cases:	(54)	(364)	(42)	(400)
Not allowed to marry	65	65	41	55
Too many rules and regulations	35	22	17	23
A life-long commitment is required	40	30	16	24
(if male:) Would you be seriously interested in becoming an ordained priest if celibacy were not required? ("yes")	36	17	a	26
(if male:) Would you be seriously interested in becoming a permanent deacon at some time? ("yes, now or later")	39	50	a	63

a = too few cases.

adults. One was composed of administrators of lay ministry training programs.

Comparing Latinos and Non-Latinos

Throughout the data analysis, we inspected differences between Latinos and all others. The differences turned out to be small. See Table A.2, which displays the items with biggest Latino-versus-non-Latino differences. The Latino respondents were more interested in considering lay ministry than other Catholics, partly because they did not have other occupations as clearly in mind. Otherwise the differences shown in the table are not very distinct.

References

D'Antonio, William V., James D. Davidson, Dean R. Hoge, and Mary L. Gautier. *American Catholics Today.* Lanham, MD: Rowan & Littlefield Pub, Inc., 2007.

Davidson, James D. *Catholicicsm in Motion: The Church In American Society.* Liguori, MO: Ligouri Publications, 2005.

DeLambo, David. *Lay Parish Ministers: A Study of Emerging Leadership.* NY: National Pastoral Life Center, 2005.

Ford, Ita, M.M. Personal letter to her niece. August, 1980.

"Frequently Requested Catholic Church Statistics." Center for Applied Research In the Apostolate (CARA). Georgetown: CARA, 2007.

Hoge, Dean R. *Experiences of Priests Ordained Five to Nine Years.* Washington, DC: National Catholic Education Association, 2006.

_____. *Future of Catholic Leadership: Responses to the Priest Shortage.* Kansas City: Sheed & Ward, 1987.

Hoge, Dean R. and Jacqueline E. Wenger. *Evolving Visions of the Priesthood.* Collegeville: Liturgical Press, 2003.

Lakeland, Paul. *Catholicism at the Crossroads: How the Laity Can Save the Church.* NY: Continuum, 2007.

United States Conference of Catholic Bishops. *Co-Workers in the Vineyard of the Lord: A Resource for Guiding the Development of Lay Ecclesial Ministry.* Washington, DC: USCCB, 2005.

Wuthnow, Robert. *After the Baby Boomer: How Twenty Somethings Are Shaping the Future of American Religion.* Princeton: University Press, 2007.

About the Project

From 2003 through 2008, the Emerging Models of Pastoral Leadership Project, a collaborative effort of six national organizations, funded by the Lilly Endowment, Inc., conducted national research on the current and new models of parish and pastoral leadership. Their objective was to find best practices and ideas of parish leadership in order to share them with pastoral leaders across the country. To round out this study, it was decided to look at the future of pastoral leadership and attempt to get an understanding of the next generation of pastoral leaders. This study, along with the attending commentaries, is the result of this initiative.

The six partner organizations of the Emerging Models of Pastoral Leadership Project are the following:

- National Association for Lay Ministry
- Conference for Pastoral Planning and Council Development
- National Association of Church Personnel Administrators
- National Association of Diaconate Directors
- National Catholic Young Adult Ministry Association
- National Federation of Priests' Councils

About the Authors

The late Dean R. Hoge, Ph.D., professor of sociology at The Catholic University of America, is recognized as a leading researcher of American religious life. Author of extensive studies of Catholicism, priesthood, ministry, and young adults, he was the lead researcher and analyst of the Emerging Model's study of the next generation of pastoral leaders.

Marti R. Jewell, D.Min., served as the director of the Emerging Models of Pastoral Leadership Project from 2003 through the completion of the first phase of the Project in 2009. Now an assistant professor of theology in the School of Ministry at the University of Dallas, she offers keynotes and workshops on the findings of the Project, addressing key ministry issues across the country.

Four more books available in the Emerging Models of Pastoral Leadership series . . .

Shaping Catholic Parishes

Pastoral Leaders in the 21st Century

Edited by Carole Ganim

Paperback • 192 pages • ISBN: 978-0-8294-2646-5 • $11.95

Shaping Catholic Parishes looks at the dramatic changes taking place in Catholic parish life from the pastoral leader's point of view. 22 priests, deacons, religious, and lay people share first-person accounts of their experiences serving as pastoral leaders in these new situations and roles. Their inspiring and instructive stories will deepen your understanding of the unique challenges facing 21st century parishes today.

LOYOLAPRESS.
A JESUIT MINISTRY

Phone: 800-621-1008 • Fax: 773-281-0555 • Visit: www.loyolapress.com/store

Parish Life Coordinators

Profile of an Emerging Ministry

Kathy Hendricks

Paperback • 120 pages
ISBN: 978-0-8294-2648-9
$11.95

With the growing shortage of priests in the United States, a significant number of parishes are being entrusted to religious, deacons, and lay pastoral leaders. Sometimes called parish life coordinators (PLCs), these men and women are bringing new life and purpose to parishes. *Parish Life Coordinators* explains how the PLC model works, shares best practices from parishes using the model, and offers practical implementation ideas that will help parishes without a priest successfully serve the ever-increasing pastoral needs of their people.

LOYOLA PRESS.
A JESUIT MINISTRY

Pastoring Multiple Parishes

Mark Mogilka
and Kate Wiskus

Paperback • 192 pages
ISBN: 978-0-8294-2649-6
$11.95

Nearly half of U.S. parishes and missions currently share their pastor with another parish or mission. In *Pastoring Multiple Parishes*, Mark Mogilka and Kate Wiskus share with readers what works and what doesn't when parishes must share a pastor, offering practical advice to help Catholics see this growing trend as a wonderful opportunity for future stability and growth of the faith.

LOYOLA PRESS.
A JESUIT MINISTRY

The Changing Face of Church

Emerging Models of Parish Leadership

Marti R. Jewell
and David A. Ramey

Paperback • 176 pages • ISBN: 978-0-8294-2647-2 • $11.95

Based on the experiences of more than 500 of today's pastoral leaders in the Catholic Church, *The Changing Face of Church* documents the best practices for approaching the massive, rapidly evolving challenge of providing for vibrant parish life. A hopeful view of the Church's future and its leadership comes through clearly from those who were interviewed for this book, and the book's you–can–do–it–too message is sure to bolster readers in their own pastoral planning efforts.

LOYOLA PRESS.
A JESUIT MINISTRY